*This book is dedicated to the memory of
Dr. Robert B. Rutherford, Jr. ~ my advisor, mentor, and friend.*

*His guidance, knowledge, and support helped shape the path
of my professional career and accomplishments.*

Challenging Classroom Behaviors:

Overcoming Resistance through Uniquely Audacious Interventions

by
John W. Maag, Ph.D.

DUDE PUBLISHING
A Division of
National Professional Resources, Inc.
Port Chester, New York

Publisher's Cataloging-in-Publication
(Provided by Quality Books, Inc.)

Maag, John W., 1956-
    Challenging classroom behaviors : overcoming
resistance through uniquely audacious interventions / by
John W. Maag.
        p. cm.
        Includes bibliographical references.
        ISBN 978-1-935609-667

        1. Classroom management. 2. Problem children--
Education. 3. Problem children--Behavior modification.
I. Title.

LB3013.M33 2012   371.102'4
                           QBI12-600103

Acquisitions Editors: Helene M. Hanson, Lisa Hanson
Production Editor, Cover Design: Andrea Cerone,
National Professional Resources, Inc., Port Chester, NY

Dude Publishing
A Division of National Professional Resources, Inc.
25 South Regent Street
Port Chester, New York 10573
Toll free: (800) 453-7461
Phone: (914) 937-8879

Visit our web site: www.NPRinc.com

Printed in the United States of America

ISBN 978-1-935609-66-7

Table of Contents

From the Author:

My professional biography is printed in the back of this book, but I'd like to share a more personal account of my background up front to give you a better idea of where I'm coming from and how I developed the strategies you will learn about in this book.

I began teaching high school students with behavioral disorders and learning disabilities when I was 24 years old. I naively harbored the belief that these students would follow all my directions because I was young and cool. I quickly learned that it was their job to be noncompliant and get my goat at every opportunity. Many nights during that first year of teaching I would drive home and replay some negative and ineffectual interaction I had with a student that day. I would literally slap my forehead—as if I should have had a V8—and say aloud to the dashboard of my car, "I can't believe the way I responded to that kid. Of the 100 worst ways to respond, I went with number 101!" For me, learning how to deal effectively with students' noncompliance was necessary in order to simply survive, let alone thrive, in my role as teacher.

My next job was teaching children with autism, schizophrenia, and other developmental disabilities. These children experienced some level—usually moderate to severe—of cognitive impairment. How difficult could it be, I thought, to deal with their behavior? By this time I had experience working with high school students and was confident that no child with cognitive impairments could outwit me. I was wrong. Instead of diminishing, my naiveté increased. These students' behaviors were dramatically different from those displayed by the high school students I had previously taught. They had their own unique ways of being oppositional. I quickly learned that just because they had some level of cognitive impairment, these students were by no means stupid. The only person that I initially thought was stupid in that classroom was me. Yet once again, driven by the need for self-preservation—and with the help of many others, including my advisor and mentor, Dr. Robert B. Rutherford, Jr.—I learned how to manage my students' behaviors, and had some amazing successes.

I next took a position as a teacher at an adolescent psychiatric hospital in Phoenix, Arizona. I began shifting my emphasis from teaching to psychotherapy, and pursed a degree in the latter. After completing a master's degree, I was promoted to clinical supervisor. The teenage patients at the facility were, as a whole, bright and extremely manipulative—in some instances frighteningly so. I am convinced that I learned much more from them than I taught them. At that time, I began studying the therapeutic work of Milton H. Erickson, MD (not to be confused with Erik Erikson, the developmental psychologist who wrote *Identity: Youth and Crisis*). Dr. Milton Erickson's amazing and nontraditional approach to psychotherapy fascinated me. I immediately began thinking about how his techniques could be adapted for teachers of students with truly challenging behaviors.

Three years later, bolstered with a wealth of experiences, I left the psychiatric hospital to obtain my doctorate. I continued studying the work of Milton Erickson as I pursued my PhD. After graduating and spending a year at the University of Maryland, I joined the faculty at the University of Nebraska-Lincoln. I also obtained two licenses in Nebraska to practice psychotherapy, which I did part-time while teaching courses and developing my research agenda. As a psychotherapist in private practice, I again encountered resistance when working with families. Families have a unique ability to maintain homeostasis and engage in a variety of counterproductive behaviors to maintain consistent patterns of interaction. Yet again, I discovered a new form of resistance.

Shortly after moving to Lincoln, Nebraska, my first son, Dylan, was born. I rearranged my university schedule so that I taught at night and cared for him during the day while his mother worked. This schedule continued while I simultaneously developed a part-time private practice. All told, Dylan was a very easy child to raise. Then, three years later, my second son, Colton, was born. I went back to teaching during the day and was fortunate enough to receive sufficient invitations for speaking engagements and consulting jobs to allow the boys' mother to stay home with them. As easy as Dylan was, Colton was not. His temperament was 180° different from Dylan's. Consequently, my initial parenting efforts with Colton failed miserably. I seemingly, and logically, believed that the parenting style I used with Dylan would be equally effective with Colton. It was Colton who taught me to adapt my parenting style to meet his unique personality. Years later, a teacher at one of my seminars handed me a piece of paper that said, "If a parent asks a child to do something 100 times and the child refuses, who's the slow learner?"

That brings me to the present. Today, I have two teenage boys and an ex-wife, which make me an expert on managing resistance. So, now you have my unofficial, but authorized, biographical sketch. The takeaway: If what you're doing isn't working, try something else—even if others think you're crazy.

Cecil's Trip

After the bell rings, Cecil saunters over to his desk, deliberately knocking several books off a shelf along the way and glaring at you challengingly. Your first thought is, "Oh no, it's going to be one of those days." Ignoring Cecil for the moment and hoping he won't ruin another math lesson, you pass out an assignment consisting of 25 problems and instruct students to begin working. Cecil finally sits down and gets out his pencil—only to dramatically break it before completing the first problem. He then sits back, flipping his broken pencil in the air. When you ask him what he's doing, he replies, "Nothing." The other students in the class have now stopped working and are alternately staring at you and Cecil. He gets up to sharpen his pencil.

The giggles begin and grow louder as Cecil sharpens his pencil down to a stub. He then opens the compartment containing the pencil shavings only to have them spill on the floor. He apologizes sarcastically as he bends down to clean them, nonchalantly stepping on a student's foot. As he begins to stand, he purposely bumps his arm against another student's elbow, causing that student's pencil to tear his worksheet. The student glares at Cecil, but Cecil just gives him the finger and says "f- off" under his breath as he walks back to his desk.

Sighing uncomfortably, you begin circulating throughout the classroom, providing students with assistance. You apprehensively glance over at Cecil who, thankfully, appears to be working. You are relieved that you can ignore him for the moment. After several minutes, you reluctantly stop in front of his desk only to discover that instead of working on his math assignment, he is writing "math sucks" all over his worksheet. With your best "teacher voice," you sternly demand that he stop writing those words and begin his assignment. Cecil looks up at you and says, "Make me!"

You are angry and frustrated because Cecil's challenging behaviors prevent you from keeping an orderly classroom and teaching the necessary content. How do you handle Cecil and others like him?

This book will help you understand the reasons behind students' challenging behaviors and why traditional techniques for gaining compliance often fail. It will also challenge you to explore the reasons for your own resistance, and will suggest ways of overcoming this resistance by trying the unconventional and audacious techniques presented in this book.

WARNING!

Before you proceed, I must warn you that the techniques for managing resistance presented in this book are audacious and peculiar. For example, one way to deal with Cecil is to demand that he not write a single answer to the problems on the math assignment! Another option is to tell him that you know he can get even better at writing "math sucks" and are pleased that he now has the opportunity to practice this skill. These two suggestions may seem pretty outrageous. After all, why would you *not* want Cecil to finish his math assignment and *continue* writing "math sucks"? The answers will become apparent as you read on. But be prepared for unconventional techniques that often include elements of surprise and shock, and have the potential effect of derailing students from their typical ways of responding to directions. Remember that these students have become experts at thwarting directions—such opposition calls for a peculiar response! Students, teachers, administrators, and parents may think you've gone a little crazy when you begin using these techniques. But that's okay. You'll learn how to handle their resistance, too.

I don't suggest abandoning all conventional techniques. Rather, I want you to ask yourself, "Is what I'm doing working?" That is, are you getting the desired response from the student? With the most noncompliant students, the answer is probably negative. Otherwise, if it isn't broken, don't fix it.

It has been my experience that teachers who appreciate, catch on, and develop their own unique techniques are able to do so because they are capable not only of thinking outside the box, but also of thinking within a completely new box. These teachers respond to resistance with good-natured humor, are not afraid to laugh at themselves, and engage with students personally—without personalizing students' behaviors.

It has also been my experience that some teachers instantly have a negative gut reaction when presented with unconventional techniques. These teachers may feel threatened when presented with any information that challenges their pre-existing notion of how to manage students' resistance. At times, it seems some teachers would prefer for their students to continue misbehaving rather than take the risk themselves of trying a new way of responding to these students. I've also heard teachers say with resignation, "I've tried everything and nothing works." I personally have been working with kids with behavior problems for the past 20 years as a teacher, therapist, and consultant, and I can say, without a doubt, that I haven't tried "everything." How would one even know when "everything" has been exhausted?

One final word about the approaches found in this book: They are no substitute for well conceived, well organized, and well implemented school-wide positive behavior support and classroom management systems—typically thought of as Tier I and Tier II interventions. Rather, they work best for those face-to-face power struggles you encounter with individual students—what would generally be called Tier III interventions.

I hope you will examine these strategies with a critical and skeptical eye. If what you are currently doing to manage students' resistance is working, put this book down and keep doing it! But, if what you are doing isn't working for some students, then read on, because besides being peculiar, these techniques also offer hope.

Learning is not doing; it is changing what we do.
—B.F. Skinner

"Each person is a unique individual. Hence, psychotherapy should be formulated to meet the uniqueness of the individual's needs, rather than tailoring the person to fit the Procrustean bed of a hypothetical theory of human behavior."
—Milton H. Erickson, M.D.

Chapter 1
The Strategic Approach and Underlying Principles

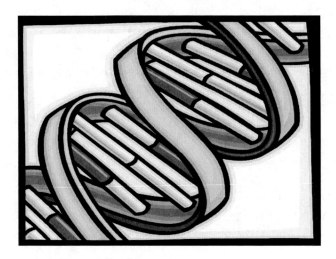

One of the most irksome experiences educators face is dealing with noncompliant, disobedient, uncooperative, and oppositional students. Techniques for dealing with these students typically target the students' behaviors, which are routinely seen as the source of the problem. However, as Hill Walker and his colleagues insightfully noted,

> *Whether or not a child complies with an adult directive has as much to do with how the command is framed and delivered as it does with the consequences, or lack of them, that follow the delivery. (1995, p. 399)*

This statement gets to the crux of the matter: The ways in which teachers behave toward students can either exacerbate or alleviate students' problem behaviors.

The strategic approach behind the techniques for overcoming resistance presented in this book draws on several theories, including B.F. Skinner's operant behavioral theory, the theory of communication developed by anthropologist Gregory Bateson, applied principles developed by Paul

Watzlawick, and the therapeutic use of persuasive language developed by psychiatrist Milton Erickson. They are premised on the understanding that human beings alter their behavior in response to the ever-changing situations they encounter; therefore, by manipulating situational components, teachers can shape student behavior and achieve compliance. Psychotherapist Virginia Satir developed her highly effective model of conjoint family therapy on the basis of this premise.

When teachers are faced with noncompliant students who consistently misbehave, they often feel as though they are engaged in a battle that requires them to push back against students' inappropriate behaviors. Although this response is rarely effective, teachers sometimes don't know how else to respond. Fortunately, all students communicate how to deal with them effectively through their verbal and nonverbal behaviors. The key to capitalizing on students' cues is to astutely and patiently observe them. Most teachers think they are alert to everything that goes on in their classrooms when in reality they miss many important student cues because they have fallen into routine ways of observing the class.

The Sailor Metaphor

The strategic teacher can be likened to an expert sailor on the open sea who tries to anticipate and plan his actions in accordance with the conditions of the wind and the tides at any particular moment. He relies on his operative knowledge to guide him in responding to unexpected events. In other words, the strategic sailor has at his disposal a range of highly flexible and adaptable tactics upon which he can draw in a variety of situations. Through his experiences, he has learned to select the most suitable and appropriate tactics to reach specific targets and solve particular types of problems. He also knows how to correct or adjust his methods as necessary.

Like the strategic sailor responding to conditions on the sea, the strategic teacher responds to oppositional students by selecting the approach that is best suited for the particular behavior, student, and situation. The strategic teacher deliberately uses persuasive communication in order to seamlessly guide oppositional students to adopt a new perspective which, in turn, will alter their interpretation of, and response to, situations.

> *I am always doing that which I cannot do, in order that I may learn how to do it.*
>
> —Pablo Picasso

Although many of the techniques presented in this book may seem odd, they have not simply been plucked out of thin air. They are based on eight principles that are theoretically important for managing resistance.

Principle One: Teacher Behavior Influences Student Behavior

About 90 to 95% of students who attend public school are generally well behaved. When these students behave inappropriately, they usually respond positively to mild, traditional forms of discipline. Most adults can remember being in school and receiving a verbal reprimand from a teacher, such as being told, "Stop talking and get to work!" In addition to verbal reprimands, traditional methods of discipline that are usually effective include keeping students after class to complete work, having them sit in a quiet chair, or taking away privileges.

Students for whom traditional interventions are effective are usually internally motivated and do not require many tangible rewards. Their parents communicate to them the expectation that they follow their teacher's directions, regardless of how other students behave. These students don't have substantial learning problems and therefore don't feel the need to misbehave for fear of appearing dumb in front of their peers. For these "typical" students, minor corrections or curricular modifications are usually sufficient to eliminate occasional problem behaviors.

However, roughly 5 to 10% of students don't respond to traditional disciplinary interventions, leaving teachers at a loss for how to deal with their noncompliance. Overcoming resistance in these students can feel like a formidable task—or, from a more positive perspective, a real challenge!

When an oppositional student does not respond to traditional disciplinary interventions, the source of the problem frequently lies with the behavior of the teacher rather than that of the student. This is not the mark of a bad teacher; it is simply an indication that the teacher needs to try a different approach to managing resistance.

Educators often believe that oppositional students simply need to be more stringently disciplined; however, the majority of students with chronic behavioral problems are subjected to more—not less—discipline than their peers. The fact that some students continue to misbehave in spite of traditional disciplinary interventions simply indicates that traditional discipline has not worked.

Principle Two: All Behavior is Purposeful

Human beings behave in purposeful ways in order to achieve desired results or outcomes, such as getting attention from others, escaping certain situations, or achieving a feeling of power or control. All people want to feel like they have control over their lives—it's human nature. Those who are able to make their way through life in a self-reliant, competent fashion are said to be empowered. The satisfaction that one feels after crossing a completed task off a to-do list is an example of feeling empowered.

The desire for attention is another characteristic of human nature. People seek attention in all kinds of ways: how they speak, wear their hair, dress, or show off their talents.

The instinct to escape or avoid unpleasant, aversive, or threatening people, things, or situations is also a component of basic human nature. Students will persist in engaging in inappropriate behaviors as long as those behaviors continue to serve a valued and useful purpose. Therefore, in order to effectively deal with students who misbehave, teachers need to become detectives and uncover the purpose the inappropriate behavior serves.

This detective work can be performed formally or informally. The informal approach involves the teacher following her instincts, asking herself why a student might be performing an inappropriate behavior, and teaching acceptable substitute or replacement behaviors that will allow the student to achieve the same goals. If this is done and the problem behavior continues, the teacher's instincts about the cause of the behavior were probably wrong. In such cases, the teacher would conduct a formal functional assessment to correctly determine the purpose the behavior serves. This process is described in Chapter 6.

It is important to remember that noncompliant students who consistently misbehave will continue to do so unless they learn other ways of achieving desired outcomes. This is why students need to be taught appropriate replacement behaviors that will allow them to achieve the same outcomes they achieve through their inappropriate behaviors.

Principle Three: Context Gives Behavior Meaning

Behavior does not occur in a random or unorganized fashion. Not only is behavior purposeful, it also derives meaning based on the context (situation or circumstances) in which it occurs. Very few behaviors are universally inappropriate regardless of context.

For example, running and yelling are inappropriate behaviors in the context of a math lesson, but these same behaviors are acceptable, and even valued, in the context of a basketball or soccer game. A behavior takes on a different meaning when framed within a new context or paradigm. Changing or manipulating the context surrounding a behavior sets off a domino effect that alters the meaning, purpose, and desire to perform the behavior. Many techniques for managing resistance therefore involve changing context.

The Context Domino Effect

Principle Four: Misbehavior Conveys Important Information

The ability to provoke a strong reaction from a teacher—even if that reaction is negative—provides some students with a sense of satisfaction. When the teacher gets angry in response to their inappropriate behaviors, these students feel powerful and in control. The teacher's reaction therefore reinforces the inappropriate behavior. For some students, the feeling of satisfaction derived from provoking a strong reaction from the teacher outweighs the unpleasant feeling of negative consequences. In other cases, the consequence imposed by the teacher (e.g., being sent to the principal's office or told to sit in the hallway for a time-out) is exactly what the student was hoping to achieve in the first place! If a student's goal is to escape an assignment, the "punishment" of being sent out of the classroom actually reinforces, rather than discourages, the student's bad behavior.

In order to avoid falling into this unproductive cycle, teachers need to resist the impulse to react negatively and reflexively penalize students who misbehave. Instead, inappropriate behavior should serve as a cue for teachers to put on their detective hats (see Principle Two) and get to work on solving the mystery of what a student is seeking or getting by behaving inappropriately. When teachers are receptive to misbehavior, they are able to calmly analyze and interpret the student's motivation, while at the same time denying the student the satisfaction of eliciting an angry or negative response.

Principle Five: Teacher Resistance Perpetuates Student Resistance

No teacher can make a student do anything. If a student refuses to complete a math assignment and says to the teacher, "Make me," what can the teacher actually do? Perhaps she could glue the pencil to the student's hand and physically guide him through writing answers, but that approach would obviously be ineffective—and might lead to a lawsuit.

Therefore, as the saying goes, "If you can't beat 'em, join 'em!" Rather than trying to stop students from behaving in certain ways or make them do something they refuse to do, teachers would do well to follow another popular adage: Go with the flow!

Jay Haley (1973) used the analogy of a man trying to change the course of a river to describe Milton Erickson's notion of the futility of resistance, writing:

> *If he opposes the river by trying to block it, the river will merely go over and around him. But if he accepts the force of the river and diverts it in a new direction, the force of the river will cut a new channel. (p. 24)*

Principle Five requires teachers to keep in mind Principle Two, which states all behavior is purposeful. The student who repeatedly acts out in oppositional ways comes to expect—and desire—a certain response (usually a power struggle) from his teacher. Responding in an unexpected manner, such as agreeing with the student or thanking him for his behavior, will preclude a power struggle. An unexpected response also prevents the teacher from inadvertently reinforcing oppositional behavior because the student is denied the response he is looking for.

Take the example of the student who refuses to complete his math assignment and tells the teacher, "You can't make me." An atypical and unexpected response would be for the teacher to say, "You're right. I can't make you complete the assignment. In fact, I refuse to let you complete even one problem!" This reaction blindsides the student and puts him in a bind. If he tries to force the teacher into a power struggle by doing the opposite of what he is told, he will have to complete at least part of the assignment—which is what the teacher wanted from him in the first place! On the other hand, if he maintains his position and refuses to complete the assignment, he will be in compliance with the teacher. Once a student complies with one request, it is easier to get him to comply with subsequent requests because of the phenomenon of compliance momentum. By providing positive reinforcement, such as saying, "Thank you for following my directions. This is a real breakthrough, and I know you'll be able to follow more directions in the future," the teacher can build compliance momentum, which is discussed at greater length in Chapter 4. She thereby increases the likelihood that the student will comply again in the future. This response will leave the student confused, but it will also set him up for future compliance.

Principle Six: Unexpected Responses Break Patterns of Resistance

One of the reasons Principle Five works so well is that students do not expect their teachers to agree with them when they are being oppositional. There are many creative and unexpected ways teachers can respond to inappropriate behavior that will help break students' patterns of resistance. Unexpected responses are useful in dealing with resistance because they throw students for a loop. After all, it's difficult for students to be resistant when they are confused and can't predict how the teacher will respond.

Sometimes, doing the unexpected means trying peculiar, audacious, and unconventional responses. The following is an example of how one teacher responded to an oppositional high school student in an unexpected and audacious way.

The new teacher was nervous as she called role. When she finished, she asked if there were any students whose names she had not called. A tough-looking boy who was leaning back in his chair in the rear of the room looked up and said, "Yeah, you didn't call my name." "And what is your name?" inquired the teacher. The boy looked at her and said, "F#@k you." There was a collective gasp before a hush fell over the room as students looked back and forth several times from the teacher to the student. Without changing her expression, the teacher asked, "Is 'You' your first name or your last name?"

This unexpected response caught the student off guard and defused his desire to be confrontational.

Responding in an unconventional way requires teachers to be aware of different options. All teachers possess the knowledge to manage resistance effectively, but they often don't realize it. The trick is to understand the difference between *knowledge* and *knowing*—the latter is much more important than the former! Knowing when an unconventional response is in order is the most valuable knowledge a teacher can possess.

Principle Seven: One Size Does NOT Fit All!

At the start of the school year, teachers often tell a new group of students to expect that they will all be treated the same way in the classroom. The purpose of this is to reassure students that the teacher will be fair and unbiased; however, this statement is counterproductive for two reasons. First, it is simply impossible to treat every student the exact the same way because no two human beings are exactly the same. A longitudinal study by Stella Chess and Alexander Thomas (1984) showed that parents who tried to treat each of their children in exactly the same way were less effective at managing their children's behavior than were parents who adapted their parenting style according to the particular temperament of each child. The second reason it is counterproductive for teachers to try to treat all students the same is that doing so makes it difficult, if not impossible, to successfully use the peculiar techniques presented in this book. If a teacher tells her students at the beginning of the year that she will treat all of them the same, then they are bound to object if she responds to one particularly difficult student in an unexpected and novel way.

Rather than telling students that they will all be treated the same, teachers should explain to students that they will be treated as individuals. For example, a teacher might announce to the class, "I'm going to treat each of you differently because I respect the fact that each of you has wonderfully diverse qualities." This statement acknowledges the inevitable—that students will not always be treated the same—and also gives the teacher the freedom to use different, peculiar approaches with different students.

Even students who have not explicitly been told to expect the same treatment may at first complain when one student in the class gets different or "special" treatment. When this happens, the teacher can assure the students that she will come up with unique and peculiar responses for each of them the next time they have trouble following directions.

Most experienced teachers realize it is virtually impossible to manage resistance with a one-size-fits-all model, and that managing resistance requires them to be flexible in the ways in which they respond to students.

Some teachers, however, are as concerned about "fairness" as are their students. These teachers think that in order to be fair they must treat all students the same. However it is absurd to liken fairness to equality, as the following story illustrates:

> *Three people in pain enter the emergency room of a hospital. A man has a headache, a woman is experiencing labor pains, and a boy is in pain from a broken ankle. The physician, wanting to be extremely fair, gives all three people two aspirin and sends them home.*

Each student is a unique individual, and teachers should embrace this diversity and demonstrate this in the ways they respond to students.

Individualized techniques for managing resistance should be developed to meet students' unique needs. There is nothing unfair about this. Equity does not equal equality!

Fair is a place where you take a pig to be judged.

Principle Eight: Compliance Begets Compliance

Common sense suggests that resistant students are more likely to perform small, simple tasks than large, complex ones. Likewise, students are more likely to follow directions that require them to do something they enjoy than those that require them to do something they dislike.

When students refuse to comply with directions, teachers tend to assume that these students are being willfully resistant or oppositional. This assumption prevents them from noticing ways in which students may have performed certain compliant behaviors. For example, a teacher may conclude that a student is non-compliant because he does not complete an assignment as directed. However, the teacher may also fail to recognize that the student has demonstrated some measure of compliance by completing part of the assignment.

The following is an example of a teacher overlooking compliance: A teacher says to her colleague, "I can't believe how noncompliant Ralph was during math class today. When I told him to stop poking Alice in the arm, he began flicking her ear." The teacher wanted the student to stop behaving inappropriately, and because he did not do so, she concluded he was noncompliant. However, she did not actually direct him to stop behaving inappropriately. Instead, she specifically directed him to stop poking Alice—which is exactly what he did! Therefore, the student was compliant. Principle Eight states that compliance begets compliance. If the teacher had recognized that Ralph changed his behavior and therefore technically complied with her direction, she could have built upon this success, eventually moving him from noncompliance to compliance.

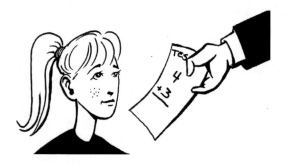

One way of establishing initial compliance is for teachers to modify assignments. For example, if a student never finishes all twenty problems on a math assignment, the teacher could "think small" and ask the student to complete two problems rather than all twenty.

Often, teachers are reluctant to make accommodations that seemingly lower the bar for students. A common objection is for teachers to say, "But I know the student is capable of doing all 20 problems." This may be true, but it's a moot point. The bottom line is that if a student refuses to work on an assignment that consists of 20 problems, there's no way for the teacher to reinforce compliance. If, on the other hand, the student is given an assignment consisting of only two problems, she is more likely to comply with the teacher's direction and complete the modified assignment. Once this first step is taken, the teacher can provide positive reinforcement to incrementally build compliance momentum until the student eventually completes all 20 problems.

Another common concern among teachers is that students who receive accommodations will come to expect special treatment, which may have the effect of reinforcing noncompliant behavior. Although valid, this concern should not prevent teachers from "starting small" to build compliance momentum. The idea is not to lower the bar and thereafter keep it low; rather, it is to make an accommodation by starting small and then raising the bar in small increments over time until it reaches the level of the original assignment. Certainly, this strategy is preferable to the alternative of continuing to insist that the student complete the same assignment as everyone else. After all, if an approach never worked in the past, there is no reason to believe it will work in the future. When a teacher has tried the same technique over and over again with no success, this is precisely the time to try an atypical and audacious new approach!

"Why do you fly outside the box?" "I fly outside the box because I can." "But we KNOW the box. We are SAFE inside the box." "That, my friend, is why I leave it. For you may be SAFE... But I AM FREE!"

Chapter 2
Understanding Why Students Say "No"

Why do children say no when adults give them directions? Teachers who face noncompliant students often agonize over this question. The most basic answer is that noncompliance gets students what they want. Of course, beyond this simple explanation, there are more complex reasons for oppositional behavior.

This chapter presents three theories of why people tend to resist changing their behavior (or simply resist change at all). These include Sigmund Freud's psychodynamic theory, family systems theory, and behavioral theory. The reasons for resistance are fundamental to the theoretical underpinnings of the techniques presented in subsequent chapters of this book.

Freud's Forecast

Sigmund Freud has been lavishly praised and fiercely chastised for his theories. Both glorified and denounced as a person, he is alternatively regarded as a great scientist, a cult leader, and a fraud. Regardless of the adulation and criticism Freud has received, few would deny the tremendous impact his ideas have had on Western culture. Freud's psychodynamic theory, which focuses on the interplay between the id (the unconscious), the ego, and the superego (social conscience), permeates modern life. Just think of all the common terms used today that were coined by Freud, from "egocentric" to "slip of the tongue" to "anal retentive." Even cartoonists evoke Freud, playing on the caricature of a client lying on a couch while the therapist takes copious and important notes!

Although some of Freud's theories failed to withstand empirical testing and/or lack practical implications, his conceptualization of resistance is quite illuminating. Why would a person be motivated to seek out therapy but then resist a therapist's help? Freud speculated that resistance is a defense mechanism that serves an adaptive function.

Resistance allows people to maintain internal equilibrium and avoid the conscious experience of emotional conflict or trauma. Those who fully comply with therapy expose themselves to the anxiety or fear associated with the issue that prompted them to seek help, thus making it likely that therapy will initially make them feel worse instead of better. Resisting therapy and repressing unwanted thoughts and uncomfortable emotions allow individuals to keep anxiety at an unconscious level which, in the short term, is less emotionally difficult than confronting it directly.

> **People don't enter therapy to cure their neuroses, but rather to perfect them.**

Family Systems: Don't Just Stay the Course

Family systems theory emphasizes relationships among members of a family, who comprise the family "system." It maintains that individuals within the system cannot be understood in isolation because they are interconnected and react to one another's behavior. Patterns of behavior develop among family members, which may lead to dysfunctional interactions. Resistance exists between individuals until counterproductive patterns of interaction are changed.

Family systems theory posits that it is difficult to make behavioral changes because people are naturally risk averse. Consequently, they try to minimize risk by maintaining homeostasis (consistency). Homeostasis breeds predictability, which in turn reduces anxiety and engenders feelings of comfort and self-assurance. The drive to perpetuate this sense of comfort keeps people locked into counterproductive patterns of behavior (another form of defense mechanism). Changing interactions is even more difficult than changing one's own behavior, because the behavior of two people is involved.

The family systems model can also be applied to the classroom, with the classroom system replacing the family system as the unit of reference. From this perspective, a student's behavior is not viewed in isolation, but rather within the context of the classroom system. To assess a student's behavior problems, a teacher would therefore look at her interactions with the student as well as the student's interactions with her and other members of the class.

Just as family members repeat familiar patterns of behavior even when it is clear that their interactions are causing problems for at least one member of the family, students are inclined to cling to familiar behaviors and routines, even when doing so makes them unhappy. Their anxiety over the unpredictable result of doing something different creates and maintains resistance. For example, students may complain about not having enough friends,

---

A Boy's Behavior Maintains His Parents' Behavior

A teenage boy had always been well behaved until his parents developed marital problems and stopped communicating except to argue. The only time the couple communicated without arguing was when boy misbehaved. Each time he engaged in some inappropriate, high-risk behavior, such as staying out past curfew, skipping school, running away, or shoplifting, his concerned parents were compelled to cast aside their differences in order to deal with his delinquency. Although his behavior got him into trouble, it also caused his parents to stop fighting, which was what he wanted more than anything. For the boy, the behavior was effective: it served the purpose of stopping his parents from fighting. The boy is unlikely to stop misbehaving unless this reinforcing pattern is broken.

---

wanting more money, or being bored, yet they will resist suggestions that they try something new like join a club, apply for a job, or develop a hobby, because any new behavior or endeavor exposes them to the risk of rejection or failure. When the risk is calculated as being greater than the potential benefit, people remain stuck in unproductive behaviors and interactions.

Another classroom example is a student who elicits a predictable response from her teacher by repeatedly engaging in an inappropriate behavior. Although the teacher is frustrated that the student doesn't change her behavior, it does not occur to the teacher that she, too, is stuck in a pattern of routinely reacting to the student in a way that is not only ineffective, but actually reinforces the negative behavior.

Behavioral Theory: Function Over Form

Behavioral theory is based on the premise that behavior is influenced and conditioned through interactions with the environment. Every day, human beings encounter countless events in the environment, or stimuli, that prompt or cue certain behaviors. Psychologist B.F. Skinner observed that a person's (or animal's) behavior "operates" on the environment, leading to consequences that constitute either reinforcement or punishment. The nature of the consequence associated with a behavior will maintain or increase the behavior (in which case the consequence has served as reinforcement), or it will decrease or eliminate it (in which case the consequence served as punishment).

Skinner famously used an operant conditioning device now commonly known as a "Skinner Box" to teach rats to press a lever at different rates and engage in other behaviors. When placed in the box, the rat naturally explored its environment. When it happened to press a lever, a food pellet was delivered. After several trials, the rat learned through the process of conditioning that pressing a lever resulted in receiving food (a desirable consequence for the rat). Subsequently, the rat's lever-pressing behavior became purposeful (he pressed the lever in order to obtain food) and the frequency of the behavior increased as he sought more food. The use of a desirable consequence that increases a behavior is known as positive reinforcement.

Skinner was also able to increase the rat's lever-pressing behavior by programming the Skinner Box to deliver an aversive stimulus at random, such as an electric shock. The rat would not know how to respond, but would naturally seek to escape the aversive stimulus (e.g., by running around the cage, pressing his face to the wall, scratching the wall, pressing a lever). When the rat happened to press the lever, the shock stopped. After repeating this sequence several times, the rat learned that pressing the lever provided an escape from the aversive stimulus. Consequently, the rat's behavior took on a new purpose: he pressed the lever to stop the unpleasantness of the shock. This is an example of negative reinforcement.

Alternatively, the Skinner Box could be programmed to deliver an unpleasant consequence, such as a loud tone, every time the rat pressed the lever. The rat's lever-pressing behavior would soon decrease as he purposefully sought to preclude the unpleasant consequence. In this scenario, the consequence (the irritating tone) acted as punishment 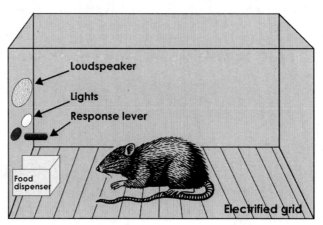 because it caused the rat to stop or reduce the behavior.

Skinner's experiments with rats demonstrate Principle Two from Chapter 1: All Behavior Is Purposeful. At the most basic level, behaviors are performed for two reasons:
    1. To obtain something or some state that is pleasurable or desirable;
    2. To escape or avoid something that is unpleasant or aversive.

Both positive and negative reinforcement maintain or increase behavior. Contrary to popular belief, negative reinforcement is not the same as punishment. In fact, it is the exact opposite. Punishment takes place when a behavior is followed by an unpleasant consequence, thereby decreasing or eliminating the behavior. Negative reinforcement takes place when a behavior is immediately followed by the elimination of or escape from something unpleasant, thereby maintaining or increasing the behavior.

From a behavioral perspective, the reasons why people resist are deceptively simple:
    1. Compliance behavior is not positively reinforced;
    2. Oppositional behavior is negatively reinforced;
    3. Compliance behavior is punished and, consequently, is not repeated.

Clearing Up Misconceptions about Positive Reinforcement, Negative Reinforcement, Punishment, and Reward

There are widespread misconceptions and confusion among educators (and others) concerning the terms positive reinforcement, negative reinforcement, punishment, and reward. This lack of clarity can cause teachers to resist using effective behavioral techniques that incorporate these concepts to manage resistance. However, even when teachers reject the strategic use of reinforcement to manage students' challenging behaviors, unplanned events that occur naturally in the classroom provide reinforcement and punishment. As a result, the behaviors the teacher would like to eliminate may be reinforced. Because of the profound implications of these concepts on behavior, they are described in greater detail below. This should help clear up any confusion and lay the groundwork for techniques presented later in the book.

Reinforcement and Punishment

Reinforcement and punishment are naturally occurring phenomenon, just like gravity. Gravity is not something that can be seen—only its effects can be seen. Isaac Newton didn't invent gravity, rather he observed its effects and developed a theory to explain it. Like gravity, reinforcement and punishment cannot be seen—only their effects can. However, teachers and parents tend to incorrectly think of reinforcement as being similar to a bribe in which a child is given something tangible, like candy, when he is compliant. Punishment is commonly equated with an unpleasant penalty or reprimand, such as spanking or harshly scolding a child. Based on these misconceptions, is it any wonder that teachers and parents are so reluctant to use reinforcement and punishment to manage students' resistance? Consider the following scenario:

> *Sally is a toddler who accidentally puts her hand too close to a hot burner. Her mother sternly says, "No!" and slaps the back of her hand. Sally cries from the pain of the slap while looking at the reddening of the back of her hand. Yet in the days that follow, Sally goes back to the stove and again puts her hand next to the hot burner, despite the fact that her mother administers the same consequence.*

The behavior in this case is Sally placing her hand next to a hot burner. The consequence is her mother saying "No" and slapping the back of her hand. Is this consequence reinforcement or punishment? Most people would say it is punishment, but that is incorrect. If the consequence was punishment, it would have decreased the behavior. Instead, it increased the behavior, causing Sally to go back to the stove and continue placing her hand next to the burner. Although Sally's mother's intended the consequence to act as punishment, it ended up acting as reinforcement. Does this mean that Sally is a budding masochist? No. It simply means that the positive emotional feeling Sally derived from receiving her mother's attention outweighed the negative physical feeling of having her hand slapped. As this example demonstrates, when people misunderstand reinforcement and punishment, they can end up promoting an outcome that is opposite to that which they intended.

Some teachers believe they have tried reinforcement and conclude that it doesn't work because in their experience it did not produce the desired results. These teachers do not properly understand reinforcement. If a teacher administers a consequence that does not maintain or increase a behavior, then the consequence was not reinforcement—regardless of the teacher's intent. Reinforcement can only be defined by the effect it has on a specific behavior.

Take the example of a teacher who wants to increase the frequency with which a shy student raises her hand to ask or answer questions during a lesson. When the student performs this behavior, the teacher verbally praises her in front of her peers. The teacher expects this verbal praise will reinforce the student's behavior; however, because the student is shy, she feels embarrassed when she is praised in public. Therefore, the student stops raising her hand—or raises it less frequently—in order to avoid being praised in front of the class. In this case, the teacher's praise acted as punishment because it decreased the desired behavior.

Conversely, a teacher's behavior may unintentionally increase undesirable behaviors, especially among students who seek attention. Often, students receive more attention from the teacher when they behave inappropriately than when they are well behaved. For students who seek attention, receiving any form of attention acts as reinforcement. Therefore, even when teachers respond in a way that is intended to punish attention-seeking students (e.g., verbal reprimand), the mere act of responding (giving the student attention) ends up providing reinforcement. Students quickly figure out that the surest way of receiving attention is to misbehave, which can lead to persistent challenging behaviors. In this way, the teacher's behavior unintentionally maintains or increases the student's behavior.

Most people aren't used to thinking about reinforcement and punishment as a result or effect. Furthermore, there is a popular misconception that reinforcement feels good and punishment feels bad. This can make differentiating between reinforcement and punishment confusing. The following example demonstrates that punishment is not inherently negative and does not necessarily feel bad.

> *A teacher instructs the students in her class to sit quietly and work independently on a vocabulary worksheet. However Bob, a student with ADHD, cannot stay put in his seat. At most, he remains seated for a few minutes before getting out of his seat to wander around the classroom and talk to himself and others. At noon, the nurse gives him his mid-day dose of Ritalin (as directed and prescribed by his physician). As a result, Bob stops wandering around and talking. Instead, he sits quietly at his desk and works on his assignment as directed.*

In this case, the Ritalin functioned as punishment as well as reinforcement. It decreased—actually eliminated—the problem behaviors (wandering around and talking); therefore, the effect of the medication on these behaviors was punishment. The Ritalin also increased the desirable behaviors (sitting quietly and working); therefore, the effect of the medication on these behaviors was reinforcement.

Reward

What about a reward—is it the same thing as reinforcement? Not necessarily. A reward may or may not function as reinforcement, depending on whether it has the effect of increasing the frequency of a desired behavior. The following example of an Olympic discus thrower makes this point.

The Olympic Discus Thrower

Several years before the summer Olympic games, an athlete began training to compete in the discus throw. During this time, his discus-throwing behavior occurred at a high rate because it was part of his training. His effort paid off and he won the Olympic gold medal—the ultimate "reward." He then decided to retire from competition. The subsequent frequency of his discus-throwing behavior decreased.

In this case, the reward (the Olympic gold medal) functioned as punishment because its effect was to decrease discus-throwing behavior. If, on the other hand, the athlete had come in a disappointing 10th place and subsequently spent more time practicing throwing the discus so he would do better at the next Olympics, then his poor showing would have functioned as reinforcement because it would have had the effect of increasing his discus-throwing behavior.

As this example illustrates, reinforcement and punishment are neither inherently good nor bad—they simply exist. They can be used effectively or ineffectively, based on the effect they have on a target behavior.

Negative Reinforcement

As indicated previously, many teachers mistakenly consider punishment to be a form of negative reinforcement. It is not. Remember that reinforcement—both positive and negative—always *maintains* or *increases* a behavior, while punishment always *decreases* or *eliminates* a behavior. Negative reinforcement causes people to perform behaviors that allow them to escape from or bring an end to unpleasant experiences, states, or conditions. There are literally hundreds of examples of negative reinforcement in daily life. In fact, the average person probably receives negative reinforcement at least 15 to 20 times during the course of a day.

The following are some common examples of negative reinforcement in everyday life:

- A car is started and the fasten seatbelt tone begins to sound every few seconds. The irritating noise continues until the driver fastens the seatbelts.
- A child whines for candy at the grocery store checkout line. In order to stop the unpleasantness of the whining, the child's parent buys her the candy.
- A blaring alarm clock goes off at 6 a.m. To stop the disruptive sound, the person turns off the alarm clock.
- A dog barks in the house. Its owners know this means the dog wants to go outside so they let it out in order to stop the barking.
- A child is walking to school. Suddenly, a hard rain starts to pound down on her. To escape the rain, she walks faster.

Ever notice the harder it rains, the faster we walk?

To some children, the classroom is an unpleasant environment from which they want to escape. Common reasons students find classrooms unpleasant include:

- Their lack of prerequisite skills to do the required work;
- Work that seems boring or irrelevant;
- Being teased in class by peers;
- Feeling like the teacher makes too many demands.;
- Interactions with the teacher that are primarily negative or punitive.

Often, students who want to get away from the unpleasant classroom environment resist or exhibit oppositional behaviors because they know that the consequence for behaving inappropriately is removal from the classroom. Therefore, when teachers remove disruptive or disobedient students from the classroom, those students end up getting exactly what they want! The consequence, which was meant to be punishment, instead reinforces the inappropriate behavior. To make matters worse, removing students from the classroom provides teachers with negative reinforcement because it eliminates the disruption and chaos in the classroom, which is what they ultimately want.

Both the teacher and the student are likely to repeat the same behaviors in the future because their behaviors have been negatively reinforced. This leads to the vicious cycle of the "negative reinforcement trap."

Furthermore, removing a student from a classroom is never productive. The only time teachers should resort to this measure is when a student's behavior makes him a danger to himself or to others. Sending a student who refuses to do his work out of the classroom is simply an illogical response. After all, if the student is not present in the classroom when a lesson is taught, there is a 100% guarantee he will not learn the content. However, if the student is in the classroom—even if he refuses to do any work—it is at least possible that he will learn something, whether he means to or not. It's better to give the student a chance of learning something by keeping him in the classroom than to ensure he learns nothing at all by removing him.

Concluding Comments: Never Overlook the Obvious

Three theories as to why people resist were presented in this chapter. They all have value. Freudian theory and family systems theory offer explanations for why predictability and consistency are so important to people in their daily lives. Human beings would rather keep things the way they are than be exposed to the uncertainty and accompanying anxiety that change brings. Behavioral theory provides a more comprehensive and sophisticated view of resistance.

As important as these theories are, the cause of resistance is not always so complex. In some instances, students who "resist" simply do not have the requisite skills to follow directions and be compliant. If they don't know how to perform the requested behaviors or don't understand what is being asked of them, students cannot possibly be compliant.

The "Can't or Won't" model of resistance represented in the diagram below illustrates this distinction. "Can't" simply means that the student lacks the prerequisite skills to perform the requested behavior. If a teacher assigns a page of multiplication problems to a student who doesn't comprehend multiplication and tells him he must complete the assignment, the student is going to be noncompliant, regardless of how many times the teacher insists that he follow her instructions. Or, if a teacher instructs a student to recite multiplication tables, but he only knows the term "times tables," he will be noncompliant, because he doesn't understand what the teacher is asking of him. Conversely, a student who knows how to perform a requested behavior may refuse to comply for reasons outlined earlier in this chapter.

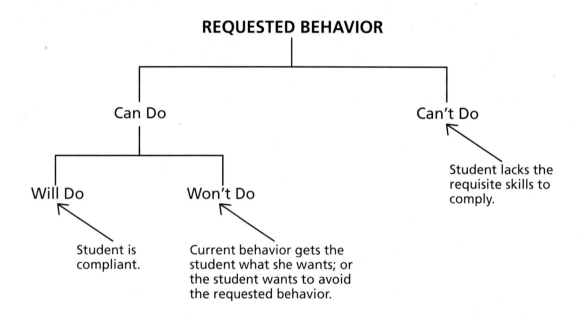

This chapter clarifies some of the reasons why students resist. These reasons also apply to adults. The following chapter offers some additional insight into why adults—in particular teachers—resist. Subsequent chapters also explain how to analyze the cause of various challenging behaviors and identify/disrupt patterns of interactions that reinforce inappropriate behaviors.

Chapter 3
Understanding Why Teachers Say "No"

When a student repeatedly engages in oppositional or inappropriate behavior in the classroom, focusing on the student alone as the source of the problem is usually insufficient. It was established in the previous chapter that behavior is influenced by interactions people have with others and with the environment. It follows that students' persistent behavioral problems are often an indication of counterproductive or dysfunctional interactions they have with their teachers. Therefore, in order to effectively address behavior problems, teachers need look at their own behaviors and interactions with students. By doing so, they may find that they are often as resistant to change as are their students.

Teachers tend to think of resisting as something students do—or, more precisely, don't do, such as follow directions. But resistance does not emerge in a vacuum. When a student resists or defies a teacher, it is the result of the student's interaction with the teacher. After all, without the teacher telling the student what to do (e.g., behave appropriately, complete a task), there would be nothing for the student to resist!

The solution for overcoming resistance, of course, is not for teachers to stop asking students to perform tasks they resist or just allow them to behave inappropriately. Rather, the solution lies in understanding patterns of interaction. This requires teachers to understand their own resistance and identify the ways in which their responses to inappropriate behavior maintain students' resistance.

The Power of Perspective

Consider the following riddles:

- *What has four wheels and flies?*
- *What do Alexander the Great and Smokey the Bear have in common?*

What do these riddles have to do with managing resistance? They help illustrate the effect of perspective.

The answer to the first riddle, what has four wheels and flies, is "a garbage truck." Before hearing the answer, most people would probably imagine some type of four-wheeled flying contraption.

Put your hands together above your head so that your palms are touching each other like you are praying. Now push with your right hand against your left one as hard as you can. Are your hands still centered over your head? If they are, you created resistance. The correct response would have resulted in your hands moving down by your left side, because you were not instructed to push back with your left hand!

The answer to the second riddle is just as obscure. What could a world conqueror and symbol for forest fire prevention possibly have in common? The answer is… their middle names! Both have the middle name "the." Once the answers to these riddles are revealed, they seem obvious because knowing the answer causes a shift in perspective.

Perspective, or *paradigm*, is important because the way an individual views the world or a particular situation affects that person's interpretation of and response to events.

Resistance Originates from Your Behavior!

When teachers are told that their behavior causes resistance in their students, the tendency is for them to refute this claim (i.e., resist). Therefore, the assertion creates resistance in the teachers. However, when teachers are told resistance originates from students, they usually agree and offer no resistance. That is because the latter statement fits their perspective, or paradigm.

Teachers' perspectives often prevent them from managing students' resistance effectively because perspective affects behavior, including the ways in which teachers respond to noncomplaint students. Perspective is therefore a major factor in whether a teacher's behavior creates, contributes to, or eliminates student resistance. In other words, teachers looking to find  the source of resistance need only look in the mirror!

Resistance and the Power of Paradigms

In his book, *The Business of Discovering the Future* (1992), Joel Barker describes paradigms as patterns or models for interpreting information. Paradigms provide a set of rules and/or boundaries within which to think and act. When someone faces a problem, that person will look for solutions within his or her familiar paradigm. In this sense, paradigms lead to "in-the-box" thinking and limit the kind of "out-of-box" thinking that may be necessary in order to find creative and original solutions to the problem of resistance.

Paradigms are remarkably strong and enduring because they act as filters for screening information. Information that aligns with one's paradigm is easily recognized and accepted, while information that is not within a person's paradigm is difficult to perceive. In some instances, data that is inconsistent with a paradigm is simply ignored. Other times, the interpretation of data is distorted to make it fit within a particular paradigm. People who maintain very rigid paradigms may actually be incapable of taking in certain data.

If the only tool you have is a hammer, the whole world looks like a nail.

Most people have seen the classic Rubin vase illustration, pictured above. At first glance, people either see two faces in profile (in black) and not the vase, or they see the vase (in white) and not the faces. The human mind has a tendency to focus attention on "meaningful" patterns and ignore other information. What is meaningful to an individual depends upon that person's paradigm.

E.G. Boring's classic young woman/old lady sketch also illustrates the effect of paradigms. Some people look at the drawing and see an old lady with a hook nose whose chin is tucked low. Other people see a young woman looking over her shoulder. This further illustrates the power of paradigms.

The following example is perhaps the most illuminating of all. When most people look at the illustration below, they see two men sitting on sofas along a hallway. The men appear to be about the same size and to be sitting in an identical manner.

However, if one were to cut the figures out of the illustration and place them side-by-side, it would be clear that the men are nowhere near the same size. The initial misperception is the result of a paradigm that "blinds" the viewer to the true visual data.

The main problem with paradigms is that they are not based on any objective data and are rarely explicitly stated. They are transmitted through experiences and culture rather than formal training. Consequently, paradigms are not challenged or held up to scientific inquiry. Paradigms exist in every professional field, even though most people don't recognize their existence.

Belief is easily confused with evidence, evidence is easily misunderstood, and misunderstanding is easily perpetuated.
— (Neale & Liebert, 1973, p. 189)

The "Back To Zero" Rule

When a paradigm shifts, individuals are sent "back to zero" and are forced to think anew. Past experiences and successes guarantee nothing.

Imagine a group of teachers at the final meeting of the school year and the principal tells them the following:

> We've had a good year and I hope you find the summer to be relaxing and reinvigorating. Oh, by the way, next fall when school begins, none of you will be using the teaching techniques you've used in the past. Rather, the district office has determined that everyone will adopt and use a new teaching method called **X-49 Sop**. We will be hiring new teachers who have already been trained in the **X-49 Sop** method to fill vacancies. I am confident that all of you will still want to teach at this school, but if you wish to do so, you'll have to change the way your teach entirely...

Would the teachers resist? Absolutely. Why? Because they are being directed to adopt a whole new way of teaching that does not fit within the paradigm they have been using. Change entails risk and therefore feels threatening and unsettling, whereas consistency provides predictability and reassurance; therefore, individuals try to maintain consistency. Cognitive psychologists refer to this phenomenon as "the concept of consistency," or "homeostasis" in family systems theory that was described in the previous chapter.

In short, people resist change because they are averse to going outside of their comfort zones. This explains why teachers often keep on using the same methods to deal with students who misbehave, even after those familiar methods have been tried time and time again and have not worked. This sets up a pattern of relying upon "linear interventions." Linear interventions are rarely effective, as the example below illustrates.

Intervention Number One: *Teacher says to student, "Stop listening to music and get to work!"*

Intervention Number Two: *Teacher repeats the direction.*

Intervention Number Three: *Teacher repeats it louder.*

The intransigency that leads teachers to fall back on linear interventions and prevents them from breaking out of old paradigms underlies a condition known as "paradigm paralysis"—a disorder of terminal certainty. Paradigm paralysis often grips teachers when it comes to the belief or paradigm that says behavior problems originate from the student and it is the student's behavior that must change. It is often the culmination of the "back to zero rule" and the "concept of consistency." In his seminal book, *Profiles of the Future,* Arthur C. Clarke (1984) writes: "It is really quite amazing by what margins competent but conservative scientists and engineers can miss the mark when they start with the preconceived idea that what they are investigating is impossible." (p. 21)

If you ask a student to do something 100 times and he refuses, who is the slow learner?

Dominant Paradigms and Their Effect on Intransigency

As stated in Principle Five, Chapter 1, Teacher Resistance Perpetuates Student Resistance. The following three dominant paradigms tend to inhibit teachers from trying new approaches for dealing with noncompliant students.

Paradigm One: Beware of Contagion

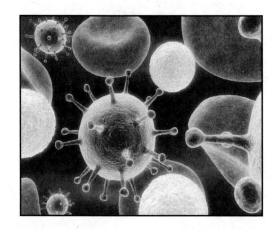

Principle Seven in Chapter 1 states, "One Size Does NOT Fit All," meaning teachers should treat students as individuals rather than treating all of them the same. However, the "rules" of Paradigm One say that when students see a peer being treated a certain way, they will demand to be treated the same way, almost like a contagion that spreads among students once they detect "special treatment" in the classroom.

For example, a teacher may resist modifying an assignment for a student, thinking, "I can't give Billy a math assignment with only 10 problems when

I'm giving the other students 20 problems to answer because then the whole class will complain that I'm being unfair and will insist that they should only get 10 problems, too." Because she believes in the contagion effect, the teacher decides she must give Billy all 20 problems to answer, just like everyone else. The result? He sits passively and refuses to complete a single problem.

Although the teacher is convinced of the contagion effect when it comes to modifying an assignment, she fails to recognize evidence that undermines the myth because the paradigm filters out contradictory information. Were she to step back and objectively evaluate the situation, she would realize the flaws in the paradigm. After all, if contagion were truly inevitable, then Billy's classmates would have stopped working on the assignment when they saw he was not working. But this never happened, nor does the teacher expect it to. She is so locked into the paradigm that she doesn't process the facts and recognize their implications.

Consider another scenario: A student with hyperactivity keeps getting out of his seat and wandering around the room. An atypical and peculiar accommodation the teacher could make for this student would be to give him three desks, placing two desks at the front of room (one on either side), and a third desk near the back of the room in the center.

This intervention is effective because it allows the student to move from one of his desks to another without permission, on the condition that he does so silently and without touching other students or their materials. Makes sense, right? Yet many teachers would resist this intervention on the basis of Paradigm One's contagion myth, which says that if one student is assigned three desks, then every student in the class will want three desks. Consequently, the teacher rejects the accommodation and the student with hyperactivity continues to walk around the classroom and disrupt others. Ironically, the teacher doesn't worry about other students getting out of their seats and walking around the room just because one student with ADHD does—and for good reason. For all the times the student with ADHD has gotten out of his seat and wandered around the room, no other students have ever followed his lead and done the same thing. And why would they? They don't have ADHD… in which case they wouldn't want three desks! The teacher has applied the myth of contagion inconsistently, only relying on it when the scenario calls for change.

Staying within one's familiar paradigm provides an easy out when problems arise. Clinging to the myth of contagion allows teachers to rationalize that alternative interventions are not worth trying because they could backfire. This provides justification for doing the same old thing rather than going back to zero and rethinking the very premise of familiar rules and beliefs.

Paradigm Two: There's Not Enough Time!

Teaching is time consuming, and it is common for teachers to feel like there's never enough time in the school day. Nevertheless, there is a surprisingly large discrepancy between the amount of time schools allocate for instruction, the amount of time teachers spend providing instruction, the amount of time students are engaged in instruction, and the amount of time students are engaged in academic

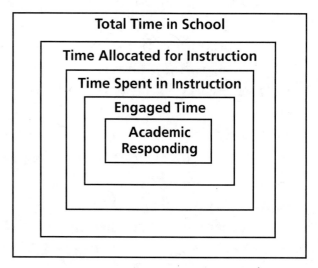

responding. Historically, it has been found that in some classrooms, students were actually engaged in instruction for only 44% of the time allocated for instruction.

As for academic responding, in some classes, students spent as much as 50 to 70% of allocated time completing independent (paper-and-pencil) or independent (non-teacher-directed) activities. When teachers assign independent activities (i.e., worksheets), students spend only about 50% of the allocated time engaged in academic responding. Even figuring in today's political realities and the additional time teachers need to spend preparing students for high-stakes tests, most teachers should still be left with a bare minimum of 30 additional minutes per day that could be devoted to making and implementing accommodations for the few students who could benefit from them, without compromising the learning of others. The impression that there is not enough time to develop accommodations is another paradigm that simply does not hold up to evidence.

The clock is ticking . . . So use those extra 30 minutes!

Paradigm Three: Control the Class

Over 30 years ago, Ken Howell described a major impediment to dealing effectively with students' challenging behaviors: the paradigm of control. This paradigm maintains that a teacher's primary responsibility is to teach academic content which requires students to be well behaved and under control. Because they naturally expect students to be well behaved, teachers often ignore students' good behavior (i.e., following directions) and focus instead on maintaining control over their classrooms by reacting to students who display challenging behaviors. Typically, this reaction consists of reprimanding or penalizing students who behave inappropriately based on the belief that such responses will allow the teacher to maintain control of the class.

Paradoxically, teachers do not reprimand students who struggle academically the way they do students with behavioral difficulties. If a student provides an incorrect answer to a math problem, the teacher does not say, "That's totally inappropriate behavior. Go to the principal's office. I will not tolerate that behavior in my classroom!" Instead of scolding the child and sending him out of the classroom, the teacher provides corrective feedback and shows him how to solve the problem.

What then explains the tendency of teachers to react so negatively—and in such a counterproductive fashion—to students with behavioral issues? It is hard to come up with a reasonable explanation—but the teacher's responses are not based on reason. Rather, they are based on a paradigm that expects students to be well behaved and "under control" at all times.

Paradigm Three leads teachers to respond proactively to matters of academic performance—devoting time to planning ways of promoting appropriate behaviors—and reactively to inappropriate behavior. Rick Neel (1988) eruditely addressed this tendency and its consequences in the following terms:

> In a reading lesson, who schedules the time of instruction, selects the material, makes the presentation, looks for responses, and then provides correction? The teacher does. When a behavior problem occurs, who schedules it, provides the materials, evaluates the response, and decides if the incident needs to go on? The student does. Who, then, is doing the learning? (p. 26)

Moving Beyond Intransigency

It is not easy to break out of dominant paradigms in order to deal more effectively with students' challenging behaviors. Paradigm paralysis has an insidious effect, undermining teachers' ability to effectively manage students' challenging behaviors. Part of the difficulty lies in the fact that the dominant paradigm to which many teachers subscribe maintains that behavior problems originate from the student. Consequently, teachers believe that solutions must be found within that same paradigm—in other words, it is the student who must change.

The key to moving beyond intransigency is being able to alter one's own behavior. After all, people don't truly have control over anyone's behavior but their own. Still, paradigm paralysis can be quite difficult to overcome. Teachers who have tried multiple strategies for dealing with students' problem behaviors to no avail are especially likely to cling to their dominant paradigms as a way of justifying the status quo rather than taking the risk of trying yet another new approach. Fortunately, there are things teachers can do to reduce resistance, such as taking the Challenge for Change.

The Challenge for Change

The Challenge for Change is a simple exercise that helps people become more flexible, less constrained by convention, and less resistant to change. It requires only very minor modifications to one's behavior and routines over a 30-day period.

Everyday, for the next 30 days, do something different!

"Doing something different" in this case does not imply doing anything drastic like taking up skydiving or scuba diving. Rather, the idea is to make consistent, small changes on a regular (daily) basis. This could mean working a computer mouse with one's non-dominant hand for five minutes; starting grocery shopping in the frozen foods section instead of the produce aisle; waking up five minutes earlier or later than usual in the morning.

The chart on the following page illustrates an easy-to-use Challenge for Change daily goal sheet that makes it easy for teachers to take the challenge. Although the changes are small, the payoff is enormous. The goal sheet may be used as is, or it can be modified to suit individual preference. It is helpful for two or more teachers (the more the better) to take the challenge at the same time. This enables colleagues to support one another and can make taking the challenge more rewarding. Teachers can make the challenge fun by competing to see who can stick with it the longest or who can come up with the most unique and bold challenges.

Making small changes every day helps teachers become less averse to change, more willing to break out of familiar paradigms, and more open to trying new techniques in the classroom. Even though the changes recommended in the Challenge for Change are quite minor compared with changing ingrained ways of responding to students' challenging behaviors, they will help generate momentum for change. This momentum makes it easier for teachers to make changes that will positively impact student behavior in the future. It's a small step, but as Principle Eight from Chapter 1 states, Compliance Begets Compliance or "think small!" Small changes beget larger changes. As Confucius said, *A trip of a thousand miles begins with a single step!"*

The 30-Day Challenge for Change Goal Sheet

	Week 1	Week 2	Week 3	Week 4
Monday	Use non-dominant hand to operate computer mouse for 5 minutes.	Write checks with black pen instead of blue one.	Use blue pen instead of black one to write one note.	Fill gas tank to an odd-dollar amount.
Tuesday	Set alarm clock for 5:55 a.m. instead of 6:00 a.m.	Mow back yard before mowing front yard.	Use different toothbrush for one night.	Buy different brand of milk than usual.
Wednesday	Start shopping in the frozen foods aisle instead of produce section.	Listen to different radio station for a day.	Watch different news station for 5 minutes.	Stir sugar into coffee in opposite direction.
Thursday	Get out of car to open garage door instead of using remote.	Take one different street on the way to work.	Say "hi" instead of "hello" to a store employee.	Buy a different brand of hand soap.
Friday	Put cheese on a different shelf in refrigerator.	Use Yahoo instead of Google for one day.	When asked how you are, say "well" instead of "good."	Shop at a different grocery store one time.
Saturday	Sit in a different chair during dinner.	Use a different glass for juice.	Memorize a new word from the dictionary.	Sleep on opposite side of bed.
Sunday	Wash whites first instead of colors.	Change the order of two books on shelf.	Smile at someone walking down the street.	Rearrange furniture for one day.

Chapter 4
Moving From "No" to "Yes:" Getting the Ball Rolling

Taking the Challenge for Change helps teachers break out of old paradigms and make productive changes, because making small changes creates a momentum for change that carries over into the classroom. The metaphor of a snowball that gets bigger and bigger as it rolls down a snowy hill, or skier who goes faster and faster as he makes his way down a mountain, illustrates the concept of momentum.

Teachers can also harness momentum to help students overcome resistance and increase compliance behaviors. This strategy is known as compliance momentum. It is based on Principle Eight from Chapter 1, which states, "Compliance Begets Compliance."

Good salespeople are usually experts at establishing compliance momentum. The one word they want to hear out of a customer's mouth is "yes," and they know that once they get a customer to say yes to some of their questions, there's a good chance that customer will say yes when they make the big sales pitch.

Consider the example of a salesman who goes door to door in an attempt to sell encyclopedias.

Encyclopedias for Sale

The salesman knows he has a better chance of selling encyclopedias to a household with children than to one with only adults. He therefore canvasses the neighborhood to locate yards with toys, bicycles, skateboards, basketball hoops, swing sets, and other objects or characteristics that indicate the presence of children. Once he finds such a home, he is ready to sell some encyclopedias!

The salesman's process might be as follows:

- The salesman rings the doorbell and a woman answers the door.
- The salesman introduces himself and says to the woman, "I'd like to ask you a few questions about children's learning. It won't take more than two minutes. What is your name?"
- While he is speaking, the salesman nonchalantly looks down at the woman's left ring finger. He notices a ring, which he expects is a wedding ring. He then asks her whether she is married, expecting she will say yes. The woman confirms she is married. Having gotten the woman to say yes once, the salesman attempts to build compliance momentum by getting her to answer yes to subsequent questions.
- The salesman's next question to the woman is, "Do you have children?" Once again, she answers yes.
- Next, he asks, "Are your children either currently enrolled in school or will they be attending school when they are older?" Whether the woman's children are too young to be in school or are already in school, she must answer yes (being homeschooled would still be considered being "in school.")
- The salesman then says to the woman, "I also have children in school. I know I want my children to do well in school, and I'm sure you want your children to do well in school, as well." The woman replies, "Yes, I also want my children to do well in school." Through this exchange, the salesman has elicited another "yes" answer from

the woman, and has also indicated to her that he shares her paradigm as a parent concerned about his children's performance in school.

- The salesman's next question is, "Do you think children who are good readers are more likely to succeed in school than those who struggle with reading?" There's almost no chance that the woman will answer no to this question, and, sure enough, she answers yes.
- Next, the salesman asks, "Do you think that children become better readers when they have background knowledge that helps them attach meaning to what they read?" The woman also replies yes to this question.

Finally, the salesman is ready to make his sales pitch. He is more confident now that the woman will say yes when asked whether she would like to buy encyclopedias, because the lead-up questions established compliance momentum. Although there is no guarantee that the woman will agree to buy encyclopedias, the salesman increased the likelihood that she will say yes to his sales pitch by first asking her a series of short questions to which she answered yes.

Teachers can use the same strategy of building compliance momentum in order to increase the likelihood that students will comply with instructions. The process begins with establishing initial compliance. Once a student has engaged in a compliance behavior—no matter how small—the teacher can build compliance momentum by providing positive reinforcement. Chapter 5 describes techniques for expanding on compliance momentum once initial compliance has been established.

Rapport

A highly effective way of promoting initial compliance as a first step in building compliance momentum is for teachers to establish rapport with their students. Rapport is created when two people communicate within the same paradigm. For example, the encyclopedia salesman created rapport with the woman when he said to her, "I also have children in school. I know I want my children to do well in school, and I'm sure you want your children to do well in school, as well." This statement indicated to the woman that he shared the same parental paradigm and that he and his customer were on the same page.

Teachers can establish rapport with students in much the same way: by communicating with them (verbally or nonverbally) in a way that is congruent with their model of the world, or their paradigm. The ways in which students communicate indicate their paradigms. Therefore, in an effort to identify their paradigms, teachers must be astute observers of students' communication. They must also be willing to respond to students in atypical ways. Consider the following example:

A teacher passes out a worksheet of 25 math problems and directs students to complete the assignment independently. One student looks at the worksheet and exclaims,

"This assignment sucks, I hate it.
I won't do it and you can't make me!"

Most teachers would consider this statement to be inappropriate and deserving of some sort of negative response or reprimand. After all, the student is challenging the teacher's authority. Typical responses would be for the teacher to say:

"If you don't finish that assignment during class,
you'll be staying after school to finish it."

"That attitude will land you in the principal's office."

"We do not speak that way in school.
Change your attitude now and get to work."

These common responses fit within the teacher's paradigm, but they run counter to the student's oppositional paradigm or frame of reference; therefore, they are more likely to increase the student's resistance than to eliminate it. A more effective way of responding would be for the teacher to indicate she shares the student's paradigm. For example, she might say, *"You're right. This assignment is stupid and I can't make you do it."*

This atypical response both creates rapport and reduces resistance. Rapport is created by the teacher who adopts the student's paradigm. It may be uncomfortable for teacher to say the assignment is stupid, but communicating this way with the student creates rapport. This response also reduces resistance because it is consistent with the student's position—he is unlikely to oppose the teacher when the teacher agrees with him!

The figure below illustrates how the process of communication between a student and teacher builds rapport.

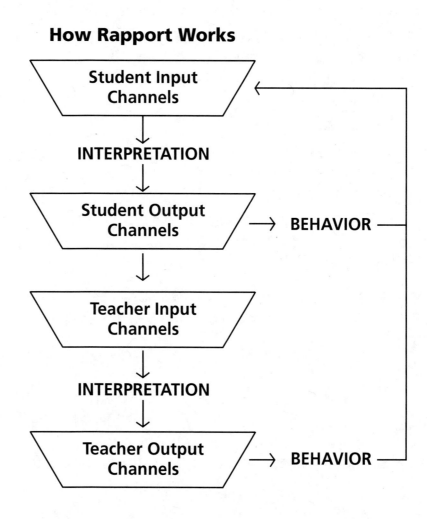

How Rapport Works

Students take in information through their five senses: visual, auditory, tactile, olfactory, and gustatory input channels. They then organize the information on the basis of their individual frames of reference, or paradigms. Their interpretation of information in turn guides their behavior (output channels). Teachers go through the same process, taking in students' behavior, interpreting it, and delivering an output (behavior) on the basis of this interpretation. Rapport occurs when a teacher's output behavior matches a student's output behavior, as illustrated in the previous figure.

Teachers who are well attuned to students' verbal and nonverbal cues can identify a student's paradigm with ease and create rapport by simply communicating with the student within that paradigm. The teacher who agreed with the student who said, "This assignment sucks," is a case in point. However, for those teachers who lack experience detecting students' cues and communicating with them in a way that establishes rapport, two specific techniques can be helpful: matching predicates and mirroring. Once teachers gain experience using these techniques, they are often able to achieve rapport without much effort.

Matching Predicates

People typically rely on one or two sensory modalities to communicate their experiences. One way for a teacher to create rapport is to match a student's characteristic use of predicates (words that imply specific action and relations, such as verbs and their modifiers) when communicating with the student. A student who communicates through tactile and kinesthetic modalities might say,

> "I know that I should have had a better **grasp** of the material, but I ran into so many **stumbling blocks**."

A student who uses visual imagery to communicate might say,

> "When everything is **clear** to me, I can **picture** the whole situation, and **see** the answers."

A student communicating through auditory modalities might say,

> "It's hard for me to **hear** what you're **telling** me, and it just didn't **sound** right."

When teachers match students' predicates, they literally "speak the same language" as their students. This signals to students that the teacher understands them and shares their paradigm. Rapport is thus established, making the teacher more credible in the eyes of students. The following examples demonstrate ways in which a teacher could respond to each of the statements listed previously using the same modality.

*"Sometimes we run into **stumbling blocks**, but it's important to keep trying. Eventually you'll **break** through."*

*"All you have to do is think about how the information **looks** and soon you'll **see** the answers."*

*"I'll try wording my directions so that they are as clear as a **bell**, without all the background **noise**."*

Mirroring/Crossover Mirroring

Teachers can also create rapport by mirroring students' nonverbal behaviors, such as their breathing rate, body posture, muscle tension, and facial expressions. Just about any nonverbal behavior that can be observed can be mirrored. Mirroring reflects students' own behavior back to them, providing an accurate source of feedback. Mirroring should be subtle enough that students are not aware they are being mirrored otherwise they may think a teacher is mocking them, in which case the effect will be to increase resistance.

An even more subtle approach to achieving rapport is to use crossover mirroring. In crossover mirroring, the teacher mirrors the student's behavior using a different body part, or output system. For example, a teacher would mirror a student's nervous foot tapping by subtly tapping his or her finger against a desk or wall. The advantage of crossover mirroring is that students are less likely to realize the teacher is mirroring them.

Both types of mirroring create rapport, which helps establish initial compliance—the first step in generating compliance momentum. Initial compliance can also be obtained through the use of Embedding Instructions and Behavioral Momentum. Embedding uses students' current behaviors while behavior momentum uses students' preferred behaviors, both of which engender compliance.

Embedding Instructions

One of the easiest ways to elicit compliance is to direct a student to do something she is already doing. Assuming the behavior is not dangerous, telling a student to do what she is already doing guarantees immediate compliance. Embedding involves interspersing (or "embedding") a new direction—something the student is not already engaged in—in between directions for the student to do what she is already doing.

For example, a teacher wants a student named Mary to open her math book to page 18. Currently, Mary is engaged in two behaviors that she finds enjoyable but that are inappropriate and distracting: shuffling her papers and talking to her classmate, Levi. The typical approach would be for the teacher to give Mary the direction to open her book. For most students, this would be sufficient; however, Mary has a history of noncompliant behavior. If she is directed to just perform this new behavior, she is likely to refuse because following the direction would interfere with what she is already doing. Such a response (i.e., refusal) would constitute entirely noncompliant behavior.

To increase the likelihood that Mary will be at least partially compliant, the teacher decides to use the technique of embedding to provide the direction. This entails issuing the direction to perform the desired behavior (open the book) in between issuing directions to do what she is already doing (shuffling her papers and talking to Levy). For example, the teacher would say, "Mary, I'd like you to shuffle your papers while you open your math book to page 18 and talk to Levi." Mary is more likely to comply with this request because it does not require her to give up the behaviors she finds enjoyable. Although she may not like opening her book, the direction seems less objectionable when it is part of a sequence that includes having her continue to do things she enjoys.

Embedding instructions in this way also makes noncompliance more difficult. Even if Mary ignores the new instruction (to open her book) and continues to do what she had been doing all along (shuffling papers and talking to Levi) after receiving the embedded instructions, she will end up being partially compliant because she will be doing two of the three things that were asked of her. Although she is not fully compliant, at least now there is some measure of compliance that the teacher can build upon to create compliance momentum.

Students who are used to resisting their teachers and who have had extensive experience with classroom interventions can be highly attuned to "tricks" like embedding. It is therefore possible that Mary would be suspicious if her teacher used embedding and would stop what she's doing (shuffling her papers and talking to Levi) to try and figure out the "trick" behind the teacher's odd request. Or, she could simply decide not to comply with any part of the directions, in which case she would stop shuffling her papers and talking to Levi and would not open her book. Either way, although Mary may not have complied with the directions, she will have stopped the distracting and inappropriate behaviors of shuffling her papers and talking to Levi. Regardless of which response Mary chooses, the result is a win for the teacher.

Some teachers worry that instructing students to engage in behaviors that are generally considered inappropriate (i.e., shuffling papers, talking to a peer) in order to get them to engage in a desired behavior (i.e., opening a textbook) will encourage inappropriate behavior. However, if a student has continued to engage in an inappropriate behavior despite repeatedly being instructed not to, the teacher is essentially condoning the inappropriate behavior. The negative consequences of persistent opposition are greater than any negative consequences associated with embedding. When other students see a classmate doing what she wants and getting away with not complying with directions, they get the message (as does the noncompliant student) that teacher's directions are meaningless.

Behavioral Momentum

Another way teachers can promote compliance is by using behavioral momentum. Unlike embedding in which a teacher instructs a student to do what he is already doing, behavior momentum involves a teacher instructing a student to engage in behaviors currently not being performed but that are nevertheless things he likes to do. This strategy is based on a very simple premise: people are more likely to be compliant if they are directed to do something they find enjoyable. When students are given directions to do things they enjoy, they will usually be compliant. Giving students several such directions therefore creates momentum, which makes it more likely they will comply with a direction to do something they don't perceive as enjoyable. The term high probability directions (HPD) refers to directions that students are likely to follow because they find the task enjoyable. Low probability directions (LPD) are the opposite and refer to directions that students are likely to resist because the task is not seen as enjoyable. To use the strategy of behavioral momentum, teachers simply provide students with several high probably directions immediately before providing them with low probability directions.

Many of the directions that are given in the classroom are low probability directions that students do not perceive to be enjoyable (e.g., "Complete problems 1 through 30 on page 67 of your math book."). To increase the likelihood that students will comply with LPDs, teachers can first issue a series of HPDs (e.g., "Take out a piece of paper and spend 15 minutes drawing."). For example, instructing a student to tack pictures on the bulletin board (HPD) and feed the class pet (HPD) before instructing him to take out the trash (LPD) creates compliance momentum, which makes it more likely that the latter direction will be followed. This is similar to the technique the encyclopedia salesman used with his customer.

The following example demonstrates how teachers can implement this technique.

- **Step 1:** Turn a piece of paper horizontally and make two columns. Label the column on the left "High Probability Direction (HPD)." Label the column on the right "Low Probability Direction (LPD)."

- **Step 2:** In the column labeled HPD, write down five to ten behaviors you know the student likes to perform. To identify these behaviors, simply observe the student and take note of what she chooses to do in her free time, or just think of all the behaviors she engages in when she is supposed to be working on an assignment.

- **Step 3:** In the column labeled LPD, write down five to ten behaviors you know the student dislikes performing. Think of the times when the student is noncompliant. What is she being asked to do at these times? These are the behaviors that belong in the LPD column. Prioritize behaviors that are practical and relevant.

High Probability Directions (HPD)	Low Probability Directions (LPD)
Tack pictures to the bulletin board.	Complete a math assignment.
Pass out papers to the class.	Read a book silently.
Draw a picture.	Write spelling words.
Run an errand within the building.	Solve a problem at the blackboard.
Get a drink of water.	Raise hand before talking.
Sharpen a pencil.	Write an essay.

- **Step 4:** Give the student two high probability directions, followed by one low probability direction. For example:
  1. "Nancy, please help me tack pictures on the bulletin board."
  2. "I'd also like you to sharpen these pencils."
  3. "Please sit down and write out the spelling words."

- **Step 5:** If compliance is not achieved, make a third column in the middle of the paper and label it "Medium Probability Directions (MPD)." This category consists of directions that the student sometimes but not always follows. Repeat steps 1 through 4, substituting MPDs for LPDs. Once compliance is achieved, incorporate all three categories of directions into the sequence. For example, begin by asking the student to empty shavings from the pencil sharpener (HPD), followed by having her collect assignments (MPD), and ending with the request to solve a problem at the chalkboard (LPD).

If the student does not achieve compliance at Step 5, simply incorporate more high probability directions into the student's routine. To build compliance momentum among the entire class, begin the day with a fun activity such as "Show and Tell" or "Simon Says" before giving a lesson on math or reading.

Conclusion

The techniques described in this chapter can help teachers initiate compliance. However, teachers must be willing to change their behaviors in order for them to work.

Above all else, teachers must check their professional egos at the classroom door. Creating rapport requires communicating with students within their same paradigm. This often means teachers saying something that conflicts with their own professional paradigm and seems counterintuitive, such as, "You're right, this assignment is stupid." Teachers should not let their ego get in the way and prevent them from doing something that goes against conventional wisdom. Otherwise, students will check it for them.

Teachers should be personal, but not personalize students' behaviors. It's second nature for teachers to respond in a confrontational way when students refuse to comply with directions and seemingly challenge their authority…teachers may take this as a personal affront. Rather than personalizing, teachers should get personal with students. This means objectively assessing students' behaviors (output) and communicating with them in a way that matches this output. When teachers judge the content of what the student is saying or doing, it is easy for them to get distracted from what is important: recognizing the student's frame of reference.

Once teachers master these mindset changes, the techniques presented in this chapter can be used as stand-alone interventions with students who are generally compliant, or they can serve as the first step in the process of expanding on compliance momentum. This process requires reinforcing compliance behaviors. The next chapter describes follow-up techniques for providing reinforcement and expanding on compliance momentum, which help students overcome frequent resistance and increases their compliance behaviors.

Chapter 5
Expanding on Compliance Momentum

Although it is almost always possible for teachers to elicit occasional compliance from any student, getting students with challenging behaviors to repeatedly comply with directions is more difficult and requires reinforcing their compliance behaviors. When students receive reinforcement for even minimal acts of compliance, they are more likely to comply again in the future, thereby generating compliance momentum. Unfortunately, many teachers take compliance for granted because they operate within a paradigm of expecting students to be well behaved. As a result, they are more likely to respond (in a negative fashion) to inappropriate, oppositional behavior than to respond (in a positive fashion, i.e., positive reinforcement) to appropriate, compliance behavior.

If teachers only respond to students when they misbehave and ignore them when they behave well, they can end up reinforcing noncompliant behaviors while doing nothing to reinforce the desired compliant behaviors. In order to expand on initial compliance established using the techniques from the previous chapter and increase compliance momentum, teachers must avoid the tendency to attend to students only when they misbehave. Instead, they must consistently reinforce compliance behaviors.

Catch Students Being Good

Any act of compliance, no matter how small, is a sufficient starting point for building compliance momentum. Once a teacher catches a student being good, all she needs to do to increase compliance is provide reinforcement, which can be as simple as verbally praising the student. This increases the likelihood that the student will perform compliance behaviors in the future.

To catch students being good, teachers need to keep their eyes open for minor acts of compliance. Examples of common compliance behaviors include:

- Sitting quietly when appropriate;
- Asking or answering a question;
- Writing an answer;
- Raising a hand and waiting to be called on before speaking;
- Lining up for recess;
- Helping another student;
- Picking up trash in the classroom or hallways.

These are just a few examples of behaviors that teachers can reinforce. The consequence used to reinforce a student's good behavior should be something the individual student finds pleasant and encouraging. For example, some students enjoy receiving verbal praise in front of their peers. For these students, public praise is reinforcing. However other students may feel embarrassed when they are praised in front of the class. Praising a shy student publicly will not reinforce her behavior, and may even act as punishment if the student stops performing the appropriate behavior in order to avoid feeling embarrassed. An effective way of delivering positive reinforcement to shy students is to praise them in private or in a note.

Catching students being good and providing positive reinforcement may seem difficult or unnatural to teachers who are accustomed to reacting to students only when they misbehave, yet the value of positive reinforcement cannot be overstated. Students displaying very challenging behaviors may need to be verbally praised as often as every minute! Many teachers are initially incredulous at the seeming impossibility and artificiality of this task, but those who follow this approach find that it makes them more attuned to students' positive behaviors. As a result, teachers find that their own concept of what is and is not possible changes.

It's really not that hard to catch students being good when first using behavioral momentum described in the previous chapter. Teachers can set up for success even for students with the most challenging behaviors by giving them many high probability directions and then reinforcing them for complying. Teachers should initially aim at giving five high probability directions for every medium or low probability direction. This approach also gives teachers practice catching students being good.

Another approach teachers can use to catch students being good is a self-monitoring card, similar to the one that follows, to keep track of the number of times they deliver praise to each of their students. This allows them to review and modify the praise they deliver, increasing praise for students who have received too little and/or decreasing praise for those who have received a disproportionate amount. In order to increase compliance behaviors, the students with the most challenging behaviors should receive the most high probability directions and subsequent reinforcement for complying with them.

CATCHING STUDENTS BEING GOOD! Place a tally mark every time you catch a student being good and provide reinforcement.					
Student's Name	Mon.	Tues.	Wed.	Thurs.	Fri.
Jane A.					
Ralph B.					
Miguel C.					
Jody D.					
Casey E.					
Nancy F.					
Britney G.					
Anne H.					
Stephanie I.					
Robert J.					
Suzie K.					
Heather L.					
Charlie M.					
George N.					

"Sure I Will"

When students are routinely noncompliant, resistance becomes a well-ingrained way of responding to directions. This pattern of responding can be conceptualized as a stimulus-response chain in which a stimulus elicits a response, which in turn becomes a cue or prompt to perform another behavior. For example, receiving a low probability direction (LPD) acts as a cue for a student to say, "No, you can't make me." This reaction by the student prompts the teacher to repeat the direction, which acts as a cue for the student to put her head down in defiance. The gesture is a cue for the teacher to administer a negative consequence, which in turn acts as a cue for the student to run out of the room or throw her books on the floor. Teaching the student to respond to directions by saying, "Sure I will" (or another compliance-based response) breaks the familiar stimulus-response chain. Once the chain is broken, the student is less likely to resort to the old, ingrained, oppositional way of responding.

Teachers can use this "Sure I Will" strategy with an individual student, a group of students or the entire class. The first step in the process is to identify for students appropriate and compliant responses to directions. This can be accomplished by providing students with an example of a compliant response to use when a direction is given, such as saying, "Sure I will!" The teacher makes sure the students know that this phrase will be considered an appropriate compliance-based response. In addition, students are given the opportunity to generate their own responses, such as, "Not a problem!" or, "Of course I will!" When students actively participate in selecting the specific compliance phrases, they feel ownership over the process and the effectiveness of the strategy is enhanced.

Once students know some appropriate responses, the teacher must make sure they know when and how to use these responses: Immediately after the teacher gives a direction, students should reply with an affirmative response. This is a universal expectation that spans classrooms and grade levels. Explain that using the compliance-based responses signals a willingness to comply with directions. To practice and reinforce using compliance-based responses, teachers can hold a contest to see who can use the most compliance-based responses (the winner receives a mystery prize).

In a perfect world, students would always comply with their teachers' directions, would always actively engage in learning, and would never exhibit challenging behaviors. But as all teachers know, the world is not perfect. It is unrealistic to expect 100% compliance by all students, all of the time. Some students (usually the majority) will be compliant most of the time. However, some will persistently be noncompliant. With these challenging students, it is best to establish incremental goals and modify expectations. This is a theme that is reiterated throughout this book.

The goal of the "Sure I Will" strategy is to elicit a change in behavior that will begin to build compliance momentum. It is possible that some resistant students will respond with, "Sure I will," only once throughout the course of a day, while other students rack up a dozen marks for using compliance-based statements. However, even one compliance-based response should be seen as progress in a typically noncompliant student. Having used the appropriate response once, there is a greater likelihood that he will use it again in the future. Furthermore, it is possible that a student might use the compliance-based response but then not follow through with actually carrying out the direction. This situation is not ideal, but the objective of this exercise is to break patterns of resistance, and even a small change, such as saying "Sure I will" without actually complying, is a meaningful first step in breaking old patterns and building compliance momentum. Later in the chapter a technique that uses a compliance matrix to promote behavioral follow through is presented. This technique can be incorporated into the "Sure I Will" strategy.

With those objectives in mind, the following steps demonstrate how to conduct a classroom-wide "Sure I Will" compliance competition:

- **Step 1:** List students' names on the chalkboard.

- **Step 2:** Each day, select a number only you know (e.g., 35, then 20, then 90) and write it on a piece of paper. On the back of a paper, name a prize. Place the piece of paper into a decorative envelope, label it "Mystery Motivator," and tack the envelope to the top corner of the chalkboard.

- **Step 3:** Explain to the class how the contest works. Tell students that you will be keeping a tally of the number of times they say, "Sure I will" (or other pre-determined compliance-based responses) in response to your directions. Show them that you will mark a tally next to their name on the chalkboard each time they use the compliance-based response appropriately (in response to directions).

- **Step 4:** Show the students the "Mystery Motivator" envelope and explain what it is. Explain that at the end of the day, you will open the envelope and reveal the secret number as well as the mystery prize. The prize will be awarded to students who have earned as many or more checkmarks as the number on the paper.

- **Step 5:** Start the contest by giving the first direction.

- **Step 6:** As soon as a student says "Sure I will" or gives the pre-selected compliance-based response, provide verbal praise and place a checkmark next to that student's name on the chalkboard. Continue recording checkmarks throughout the day whenever students give compliance-based responses.

This exercise can be easily modified to use with a single student rather than the full class. Simply explain the game to the student in advance and tell him that the "Mystery Motivator" will be in your desk drawer. Instead of writing the student's name on the board and drawing checkmarks, keep a tally of his responses on a private list at your desk, or drop a marble in a jar for each compliance-based response. Reveal the number and prize to the student at the end of the day. Because students don't know the mystery number ahead of time and because that number varies greatly from day to day, they never know when they have reached the goal number. This keeps them motivated and prevents them from slacking off just because they might know the number or if the goal were to simply beat other classmates.

Students can initially be reinforced each time they say, "Sure I will." This helps them make the connection between the teacher's direction, their responding with a compliance-based statement, and positive reinforcement. However, positive reinforcement will ultimately be more powerful when it is delivered intermittently. Therefore, once students are regularly giving compliance-based responses, they should be reinforced at random times during the day, before specific behavioral requests are introduced. Through repetition and the occasional use of reinforcement, the words "Sure I will" become habitual and are more likely to be spoken in response to a request in the future.

Compliance Matrix Games

After students have been reinforced for saying a compliance-based statement, the next step is for them to follow through and comply with the direction. Compliance matrix games offer a fun and effective way of reinforcing students for performing compliance behaviors. A simple version of a compliance matrix game is modeled after the popular game, BINGO. A group of students can play the game together, or the game can be played with individual students.

Creating a Compliance Matrix Game

The word *matrix* refers to a square composed of several equal-sized cells. A compliance matrix game requires a laminated matrix board, matrix chips, and a container in which to store the chips.

A compliance matrix game can be created by following these simple steps:

- Draw different size matrices (i.e., 3x3, 4x4, 5x5) on poster board. Number each cell in the matrix using a permanent marker. Laminate each matrix board.

- Purchase plastic poker chips, such as those available from most discount or party stores.

- Label each poker chip with a number from the matrix. Mark one chip "wild card."

- Obtain an opaque container, such as a coffee can or small box, to store the numbered chips. An oatmeal container decorated with construction paper can also be used for this purpose.

Compliance Matrices

1	2	3
4	5	6
7	8	9

1	2	3	4
5	6	7	8
9	10	11	12
13	14	15	16

1	2	3	4	5
6	7	8	9	10
11	12	13	14	15
16	17	18	19	20
21	22	23	24	25

To implement this technique with a single student, tell the student that you will be playing a game with her that is a lot of fun. Show her the matrix and explain how the game works:

- "This jar is full of game pieces. Each piece is a chip with a number on it. The number on the chip matches a number on this grid."

- "To play the game, I will give you a direction to follow. For example, I may tell you to sit on the floor cross-legged. If you follow my directions within 10 seconds, you will get to reach into the jar and pull out a chip."

- "Once you pull a chip, you will read the number that is written on it. You will then find that number on this board and will draw an "X" over that number. Then you will have another turn."

- "Each time you follow my directions you will get to pull another chip out of the jar. We will keep crossing numbers off the chart until you have a line of "X"s (demonstrate vertical, horizontal, diagonal line).

- "If you get a chip that says 'wild card' instead of having a number on it, you get to cross off whichever number you choose. The object of the game is to cross off a line of numbers, so you will want to cross off a number that will help you complete a line."

- "When there is a line of "X"s on the board, you've won the game! Once you've won, I will give you the prize that you selected before we started playing."

Make sure the student understands how to play the game. If she does not understand how to play or what is expected of her, the exercise will only lead to frustration and will not strengthen compliance. To prevent this from happening, you can have the student give you a direction and then model the correct way to follow the direction. Emphasize to the student that in order to progress in the game and ultimately win a prize she must follow your directions within a predetermined period of time (e.g., 5 or 10 seconds). Allowing her to select a prize in advance will ensure that the prize is something she values. This high-value prize will act as a reinforcer.

When first introducing a student to the game, start by using a 9-cell matrix. This sets the student up for success because the fewer the cells, the quicker and easier it is to "win" the game. After the student responds to directions consistently, introduce the 16-cell matrix, followed by the 25-cell matrix. At first, include only poker chips with numbers that correspond to the numbers on the matrix in the jar. Once the student has had gotten used to the game and is exhibiting a high level of compliance, poker chips marked with numbers other than those that appear on the matrix board can be added to the jar. This makes reinforcement intermittent and, consequently, powerful. Continuous reinforcement is desirable when first teaching a student to make the connection between a new behavior and the positive consequence. However, if a student receives too much reinforcement, she may burn out (i.e., satiate) and no longer be motivated to perform the desired behavior. When reinforcement is delivered intermittently, the student is less likely to burn out. She is also more likely to engage in the desirable behavior in order to obtain it quickly because she doesn't know when the reinforcement may be delivered. The operation of a slot machine provides a good example. Because a person doesn't know when the machine will pay off (i.e., receive reinforcement), she is more likely to engaging in high levels of the behavior (pulling the lever) to increase her chances of winning. Intermittent reinforcement works the same way for students in a classroom.

As indicated, the compliance matrix game can also be used with a group of students. This can be accomplished as follows:

- **Step 1:** Place the chip container in the front of the room next to the mystery motivator envelope used in the "Sure I Will" exercise.

- **Step 2:** Assign students to one of three or four groups. Allow a student from one of the groups to select a numbered poker chip when he or she complies with your request. Several teams can occupy the same cell if they randomly draw that cell's number. Any number of teams can win by reaching the set criterion. A student who tries to sabotage her team's effort to win can be removed from the team (the procedure can then be administered to her individually).

- To meld "Sure I Will" with the compliance matrix game (to promote follow through), continue to keep a tally of each compliance-based response, but in addition mark off a cell on the matrix when a student (or group) actually performs the behavior specified in the direction within the predetermined time period.

Chart Moves

Chart Moves is another technique for expanding on compliance momentum. A simple version of Chart Moves requires students to complete a connect-the-dots picture. Each time a student performs a compliance-based behavior, that student earns a turn to connect a certain number of dots on the picture. The opportunity to connect the dots therefore serves as the reinforcer. Students will be eager to earn turns because each series of dots connected brings them closer to completing the picture. The picture therefore serves as a visual representation of their progress, and the completed picture can be taken home as a "prize."

To provide additional motivation and reinforcement, allow students to select from a jar of mystery prizes when they complete their pictures. Another option is to distinguish several "special dots" by circling them. When a student connects to one of the "special dots," she earns a small reinforcer. Interspersing these "special dots" provides more frequent reinforcement. When the picture is complete, the student receives a bigger reinforcer.

A variation of Chart Moves that can be used with older children is the tower model. In this version, a tower or column is depicted on a sheet of paper, poster board or chalkboard. The tower is divided into multiple increments, as illustrated on the following page. Each time the student engages in a requested behavior, one segment of the tower is shaded. Various reinforcers may be awarded at specified levels, or one reinforcer may be awarded once the tower is completely shaded.

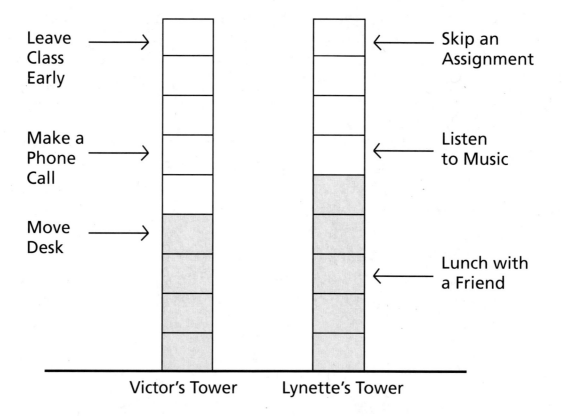

Leave Class Early →

Make a Phone Call →

Move Desk →

← Skip an Assignment

← Listen to Music

← Lunch with a Friend

Victor's Tower   Lynette's Tower

Chart Moves exercises can be adapted to almost any activity a student enjoys. For example, a kindergarten-aged student who enjoys puzzles can earn a turn to place one puzzle piece on the board each time she complies with the teacher's directions.

In fact, there are an endless number of ways chart moves can be created. The more creative a teacher can be, the more effective the chart. It helps for a teacher to find out a student's interests and develop a chart move around them. For example, if a student likes football, the teacher can draw a football field on a green poster board, mark each 10-yard line, and designate the end-zones. The teacher can get the logo of the student's favorite team and paste it at the 50 yard line.

Additional examples of Chart Moves are provided in the table on the following page.

COOL CHART MOVES FOR COMPLAINCE		
PRESCHOOL Compliance rewards	**ELEMENTARY** Compliance rewards	**SECONDARY** Compliance rewards
Mr. Potato Head: Add a facial feature	*Treasure Map:* Discover a clue	*Football Helmet:* Put a sticker on helmet
Pretty Pretty Princess: Add an article of clothing.	*Football:* Move ball from end zone to "touchdown."	*Guitar Hero:* Move from city to city.
Farm Animals: Move a plastic animal from the barn to the corral.	*Balloons:* Pop a balloon (or pretend to pop one on a poster).	*Build-a-Date:* Construct perfect date element by element.
Fish Bowl: Move a fish from one bowl to another.	*Baseball diamond:* Advance one base.	*Model:* Build a model, one piece at a time.
Apple Tree: Pick an apple from a tree.	*Board Game:* Take a turn at game, such as "Candy Land" or "Life."	*Concert T-Shirt:* Add dates and cities to a real or virtual t-shirt.
Banana Split: Add a component of a banana split (banana, scoop of ice cream, chocolate sauce, whipped cream) to a sundae or to a picture of one.	*NASCAR:* Move a toy car around a portion of the track.	*Food Drive:* Move a can of food from a collection in the classroom into a box to be donated to the hungry.
Picture Reveal: Remove one sticky note from a picture covered with sticky notes.	*Gum Chain:* Add a gum wrapper to a chain displayed around the room.	*Build-a-Guitar (or other instrument):* Add a component of the instrument until it is completed.

Spinners

Spinners, such as the kind used for board games, can be incorporated into the techniques described previously. Most school supply stores sell spinners that can be customized, or a spinner from a board game can be easily modified. Simply divide the circle at the base of the spinner into several segments, labeling each segment with a prize or privilege. Spinners can be used in the following ways:

- "Sure I Will" strategy: Student gets to spin the spinner when she responds with a compliance-based statement.

- Compliance matrix game: Student earns a spin of the spinner when he crosses off the final cell to complete a line.

- Chart moves exercise (connect-the-dots): Student spins the spinner when she connects to a special dot.

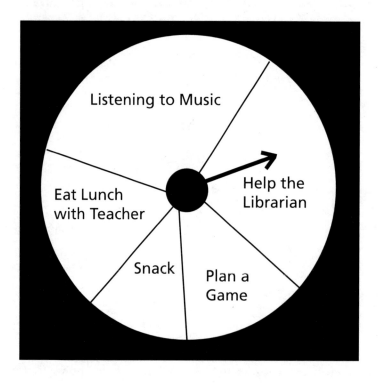

49-Square Chart

The 49-Square Chart can be used in conjunction with other techniques presented in this chapter, or it can be used as a stand-alone approach. There are six steps for creating the 49-square chart:

1. Draw a large square just within the margins of a poster board. Divide the square into 49 smaller squares (7x7). Laminate the chart.

2. Create a second chart, identical to the first, but do not laminate.

3. On the chart that is not laminated, number the squares from 1 to 49, then cut out each numbered square and laminate separately.

4. Place Velcro strips on the back of each laminated, numbered square. Place the backing for the Velcro strips on each square on the chart so that the numbered squares can be stuck to the squares on the chart.

5. Using a dry-erase marker, randomly mark several squares on the chart with an "X." (When first introducing students to this exercise, mark an "X" on at least half of the squares.)

6. Cover each square of the chart with its corresponding numbers.

49-Square Chart

1	2	3	4	5	6	7
8	9	10	11	12	13	14
15	16	17	18	19	20	21
22	23	24	25	26	27	28
29	30	31	32	33	34	35
36	37	38	39	40	41	42
43	44	45	46	47	48	49

Each time a student performs the requested behavior, she gets to remove a square from the chart. If the square revealed has an "X" on it, the student is awarded a spin of the spinner (the segment that the spinner lands on will indicate the reinforcer the student receives). Another option is to list a different reinforcer on each square on the board and provide the student with that reinforcer when it is revealed. Some squares can be labeled "pick another square."

Over time, the number of squares marked with an "X" or listing a reinforcer should be gradually decreased so that students have less of a chance of earning a reinforcer. This approach makes use of intermittent reinforcement, which is more powerful than continuous reinforcement. The goal is for students to require less and less reinforcement, until they follow directions without needing or expecting reinforcement. However, this will take time, and some students will require more frequent reinforcement for a longer period of time than others. It is important not to decrease reinforcement too quickly, otherwise this technique will be ineffective.

There are a variety of ways the 49-Square Chart can be used in conjunction with the other techniques presented in this chapter. For example, when using Chart Moves, the student may choose a numbered square to remove from the chart when he reaches a special dot or a designated level on the tower. If an "X" is revealed, the student can spin the spinner and collect the reinforcer indicated on the wheel. If working with a compliance matrix, the student may choose a numbered square to remove from the chart once he has completed a row, column, or diagonal. If an "X" is revealed, the student can spin the spinner and collect the corresponding reinforcer.

Be Persistant and Don't Despair!

Understandably, working with students with challenging behaviors causes many teachers to become frustrated and discouraged. These feelings are only natural, but they can be highly counterproductive. To avoid defeatism, it is important for teachers to focus on incremental goals and long-term progress, keeping in mind that eliciting even a small measure of compliance is an important first step in overcoming resistance.

Providing positive reinforcement to increase compliance momentum not only benefits students, but also helps teachers recognize all the ways in which students are compliant and well behaved instead of just noticing the things they do wrong. It's important to understand that increasing compliance behaviors may take time, so don't expect miracles overnight. It may take some time before highly resistant students follow directions, but be patient and stick with them because any change is always a step in the right direction!

Chapter 6
Making Use of Problem Behaviors: Functional Assessment and Resistance

Many students will respond to the strategies and techniques for overcoming resistance presented in the previous chapters; yet, for some students with severely challenging behaviors, these techniques will not be sufficient. The persistence of challenging behaviors indicates that the behaviors serve some important purpose for the student. In such cases, teachers need to determine the purpose a behavior serves and then tailor interventions to address that specific purpose. Functional assessment is a process that can be used to help make these determinations and develop functionally relevant interventions—those making use of problem behaviors. The process begins with understanding the classroom environment.

Functional assessment relies heavily, but not exclusively, on the operation of antecedents and consequences, which were introduced in Chapter 2. Recall that events and behaviors that occur in the environment before someone (or something, in the case of Skinner's rats) performs a behavior are called *antecedents*. They exist for all behaviors and serve as cues or prompts to behave in certain ways.

Consequences are events and behaviors that change an environment after a behavior is performed and influence future antecedents and behaviors. As explained in Chapter 2, consequences act either as reinforcement, which maintains or increases a behavior, or punishment, which decreases or eliminates a behavior. Consequences take two forms:

1. After a behavior occurs, something new is added to the environment (e.g., a student receives 10 minutes of free time after completing an assignment).

2. After a behavior occurs, something that is already present is removed from the environment (e.g., a teacher stops standing over a student after she completes an assignment).

The process of conducting a functional assessment involves identifying the antecedent that cues or prompts a problematic behavior and changing or manipulating it to see what impact the change has on the behavior in question. If the problematic behavior occurs less frequently or is eliminated after the antecedent is manipulated, then it can be determined that the antecedent had triggered the behavior. For students who are generally compliant, it may not be necessary to proceed with a full functional assessment, for if manipulating the antecedent eliminates the behavior, simply taking away or limiting a student's exposure to that antecedent in the future can serve as a sufficient intervention.

Antecedent Manipulation

There are an endless number of ways antecedent manipulation can be used to eliminate problem behaviors. For example, if Joey tantrums each time the teacher blows the whistle at the end of recess to indicate that it's time to come inside, she could use a bell instead or speak to Joey individually a few minutes before recess is over to alert him that time's almost up. Or, if the teacher routinely gets into power struggles with Roger after sending him to sit in a corner when he misbehaves, she could try a different response, such as passing him a note when he misbehaves that says he will be required to stay after class if his behavior continues.

Antecedent manipulation is especially useful when working with students for whom opposition escalates to aggression. It is critical to focus on prevention with students who are prone to displays of aggression, especially those who are liable to engage in behaviors that are dangerous to themselves or to others. If a situation escalates to the point where the student is violent and out of control, he will need to be removed from the classroom or the school. In extreme cases, such as when a student is hitting and spitting on others, throwing objects, or violently tearing the room apart, the police may even need to be called. While there is no therapeutic value in calling the police or removing a student from the classroom—and doing so may actually reinforce the aggressive behavior by allowing the student to escape the classroom environment—safety must always come first. However, the teacher or a team from the school should subsequently review all the factors that preceded the aggression to determine which antecedents can be manipulated to decrease the chance that the student's aggression will be triggered in the future.

The table on the following page lists several common behavior problems and offers suggestions for antecedent manipulation. Dr. Robert Rutherford, Jr., provided these examples over 30 years ago but they are still relevant and quite illustrative. A brief rationale for each is provided below.

SITUATION	ANTECEDENT SOLUTION
1. The student always fights in the lunch line.	• Move him to the front of the line, making him the leader.
2. The student comes into the room with a look that suggests he's angry and about to blow.	• Send him on an errand to the office or the library.
3. The student is too self-conscious to read aloud and acts out when it's her turn to do so.	• Arrange a "quiet corner" where she can read to you privately or speak into a voice recorder.
4. The student becomes frustrated when given a page of math problems to solve.	• Cut her paper into strips so that only a few problems are on each strip, or present her with only half of the assignment at a time.
5. The student cries when you return her paper and she sees lots of red ink (indicating errors).	• Mark the correct answers instead of the incorrect ones; erase the wrong answers and give the student a second chance to answer the question.
6. The student tips his chair back.	• Give him a clipboard so he can stand while he works.
7. The student dawdles and dislikes leaving the classroom for recess.	• Bring a special toy (ball, yo-yo, paddleball) for him to play with while gently escorting him to the door. Then hand him the toy as he leaves.

Situation #1: The student who fights in the lunch line is moved to front of the line.

Some teachers would question "rewarding" a student who pushes by moving him to the front of the line. However, if the behavior subsequently decreases, then the manipulation will have actually acted as punishment, not reward or reinforcement. Remember, punishment is any consequence that decreases or eliminates a behavior.

Situation #2: The student who comes into the room agitated and on the verge of a meltdown is sent out of the classroom on an errand to the library or the office.

Although sending the student out of the classroom may result in him missing valuable instructional time, nothing will be accomplished by allowing him to remain in the classroom when he is on the verge of a meltdown: he will not complete any of his work and will most likely disrupt others in the class who are working. Going on an errand may give him time to collect himself so that he is able to participate when he returns to class.

Situation #3: The student who is self-conscious reading in front of the class is permitted to read into a voice recorder or to the teacher in private.

The purpose for having a student read aloud is to appraise fluency. If a student can read words accurately and quickly (i.e., fluently), that skill will become unconscious and automatic. She can then allocate her conscious attention to deriving meaning from the material. Having the student read to the teacher in private or read into a voice recorder allows the teacher to assess the student's fluency, whereas no assessment can be made if the student is too nervous to comply.

Situation #4: The student who cannot or will not complete an entire assignment is given only a portion of the assignment to complete at a time.

Teachers may initially think, "I can't give her a shorter assignment because, then everyone will want a shorter assignment." This concern is based on the "contagion myth" described in Chapter 3. However, the proposed solution doesn't actually shorten the assignment, but rather cuts it into smaller segments that add up to the same amount of work. Even if it is necessary to give the student a shorter assignment, it is better to have her complete part of the assignment than none of it at all.

Situation #5: For the student who cries when she gets back a paper marked with many errors, the teacher marks correct answers and erases incorrect ones so that the student has another chance to solve them.

This solution allows the teacher to provide feedback without upsetting the student. It also has the added benefit of giving the student the opportunity to try again where she had previously made errors. If the student cannot solve the problems on her second try, this is an indication that re-teaching is required.

Situation #6: The student who tips back in his chair is provided with a clipboard so he can work from a standing position.

Some students have a hard time sitting still but will complete their work if they are able to stand up or move around. If giving a student a clipboard results in him doing his work, everybody wins. The teacher should therefore try removing the student's chair and giving him a clipboard. She should also explain to the student why she is taking these measures so the student does not feel like he is in trouble.

Situation #7: The student who is reluctant to leave the classroom is given a distracting toy on the way out.

A student may dawdle and resist leaving the classroom for recess for a variety of reasons. It is important to investigate the cause. In the meantime, providing the student with something like a special toy may distract him enough that he will respond to gentle physical prompts to be escorted outside. This manipulation can help establish compliance momentum and break the student's pattern of resistance to leaving the classroom.

The preceding situations and solutions are only a few examples of the endless ways teachers can manipulate antecedents to prevent future behavior problems. These manipulations, and others like them, require teachers to make accommodations for students who are struggling in some fashion. It is astonishing how reluctant—even resistant—many teachers are to making accommodations for students, either because of the contagion myth (Paradigm One), time concerns (Paradigm Two), fear of rewarding bad behavior, or other misplaced concerns (See Chapter 3 to review the de-bunking of these paradigms).

There is no reason for teachers to resist making accommodations for students. After all, accommodations are everywhere in society as the following examples illustrate:

- An escalator is an accommodation for people who can't climb stairs.
- An elevator is an accommodation for people who can't climb stairs or ride an escalator.
- Orthotics are an accommodation for people who walk a lot or have problems with their knees, legs, or feet.
- Different height drinking fountains accommodate people of varied heights.
- Levers that adjust car seat positions are accommodations for different size drivers.
- Eyeglasses are accommodations for people who have vision problems, just as hearing aids are accommodations for those who are hard of hearing.
- Buildings with steps also have ramps to accommodate people in wheelchairs or those with strollers.

The list goes on and on: A television remote is an accommodation (yes, people use to actually get up from their chair or couch and change the channel by hand!). So, why do some teachers resist providing accommodations? Usually, the reason is paradigm paralysis.

Why should the classroom be the only setting in our society that is free of accommodation?

Functional Assessment

Manipulating antecedents will not always prevent episodes of challenging behaviors. In such cases, or whenever a teacher wants to understand the reason for a student's persistent challenging behavior, a thorough functional assessment should be conducted. This process will help the teacher understand the purpose a behavior serves and develop effective targeted interventions.

The process of conducting a functional assessment can be broken down into two stages:

1. Generating a hypothesis of the purpose a behavior serves for a student;

2. Testing the hypothesis to determine if it is correct.

This process should sound familiar because it's based on the scientific method through which scientists first generate a hypothesis about whatever phenomena they are studying and then seek to prove the hypothesis through a reproducible experiment. Prior to developing an initial hypothesis, scientists read many articles published on the topic, confer with colleagues, and conduct pilot studies to obtain relevant data. A hypothesis is different from a guess because a hypothesis is based on research and data, whereas a guess is based on a whim or a notion. The more information collected prior to developing a hypothesis, the more likely the hypothesis will be confirmed when subjected to testing.

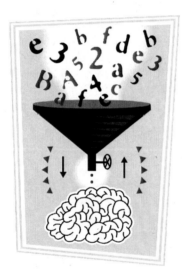

The process of conducting a functional assessment is quite similar to the scientific method. It starts with the teacher collecting global information, such as interviews with people who work closely with a student in a variety of situations, as well as psychological reports, student assistance team reports, individual education programs, and completed rating scales. The most important data (and the easiest to collect) comes from observing the student in the situations and settings in which noncompliance is most prevalent.

The process is straightforward: move from general information to more specific information in order to develop a hypothesis. Think of it as a "funneling down" process.

Generating a Hypotheses through Direct Observation

The antecedents and consequences of a student's behavior can be identified by simply looking at what happens in the environment immediately before the behavior occurs and immediately after it occurs. The easiest way to categorize this information is to divide a horizontal piece of paper into three columns, labeled "antecedent," "behavior," and "consequence," and record observations on this sheet.

This process is known as an "A-B-C analysis." When generating an initial hypothesis, keep in mind the two primary reasons why students misbehave: to obtain something they want, or to escape/avoid something they find unpleasant. As previously discussed, students who misbehave are often seeking attention. Those who misbehave in order to escape or avoid something unpleasant in the classroom are often responding to negative interactions with peers or to assignments/tasks/activities that are either too challenging, not challenging enough, or not relevant to their experiences.

The following table depicts an A-B-C analysis focused on Kevin's behavior. The activities are ordered to reflect the flow from top left to bottom right.

A-B-C Analysis

Antecedent	Behavior	Consequence
Teacher passes out math assignment.	Kevin gets out of his seat and walks around the room.	Teacher tells Kevin to sit down.
Sally starts working.	Kevin pushes Sally's elbow, causing her to giggle.	Teacher gives Kevin a warning glance.
Teacher sits at her desk.	Kevin takes out a comic book and begins to look through it.	Teacher walks to Kevin's desk and takes away his comic book.
Sally (who sits one row over from Kevin) talks to a classmate.	Kevin says, "fart knockers," while faking a cough.	Sally rolls her eyes.
Teacher tells the class to settle down.	Kevin walks to the pencil sharpener and empties pencil shavings on the floor.	Classmates watch Kevin and laugh.
Teacher tells Kevin to clean up shavings.	Kevin says it was a mistake.	Teacher walks up to Kevin and tells him to get to work or he'll stay inside at recess.
Sally raises her hand.	Kevin announces to the class that Sally is dumb.	Sally tells Kevin to shut up.
Teacher reprimands Kevin.	Kevin starts singing loudly.	Everyone in the class laughs.

Upon reviewing this A-B-C analysis chart, one hypothesis the teacher could make is that Kevin engages in inappropriate behaviors because these behaviors get him attention (from his teacher, from Sally, from other students, or any combination of the three). For some students, even negative attention, such as being reprimanded by the teacher or annoying Sally, is better than no attention at all. Misbehaving could serve the purpose of getting Kevin the attention he seeks.

An alternative hypothesis the teacher could make is that Kevin misbehaves to escape or avoid working on the math assignment. When Kevin is misbehaving, he isn't engaged in the assignment. If the teacher suspects escape is Kevin's motive, she will need to collect more information to determine why he wants to escape or avoid the math assignment. Possibilities include:

- The assignment is too easy.

- The assignment is too difficult.

- The assignment is boring.

Testing Hypotheses through Environmental and Curricular Manipulations

Just like scientists, teachers need to test the hypotheses they generate. The second stage of functional assessment, known as functional analysis, involves conducting tests (analyzing) to determine whether a hypothesis is correct. A hypothesis that a behavior serves the function of attention or escape can be tested by manipulating some aspect of the environment (antecedents or consequences) or some aspect of the curriculum (e.g., lesson format, materials, task difficulty).

<u>Hypothesis</u>: **Kevin misbehaves to get attention from Sally, from the teacher, or from other peers.**
The easiest way to test the hypothesis that Kevin misbehaves to get Sally's attention would be for the teacher to move Kevin to another part of the room, away from Sally, and then observe his behavior. There are several ways in which Kevin could respond that would support the hypothesis that

he is misbehaving to get Sally's attention. If he stops misbehaving because he is too far away from Sally to gain her attention through inappropriate behaviors, then the teacher can conclude that the hypothesis is correct. Another response that would confirm the hypothesis that Kevin misbehaves to get Sally's attention would be for Kevin to try new ways of getting Sally's attention from afar, such as throwing something across the room at her.

If Kevin continues to misbehave in ways that do not involve Sally, then the teacher can conclude that Kevin is seeking attention, though not specifically from Sally. For example, if he were to start talking to a peer sitting next to him after having his seat moved, the purpose could be to get attention from peers and/or to get negative attention from his teacher by misbehaving.

Hypothesis: Kevin misbehaves to escape the math assignment.
To test this hypothesis, the teacher would modify the assignment and see how Kevin responds. If there is reason to suspect the assignment is too difficult for Kevin, the teacher would give him an easier assignment. If she suspects the assignment is not challenging enough, she would provide him with more difficult work. If Kevin stops misbehaving after either of these modifications has been made, then the teacher can conclude that he was previously trying to escape an unpleasant situation. Now that the assignment is neither too easy nor too difficult, Kevin has no reason to want to escape and therefore no motive to misbehave—that is, unless the assignment does not interest him.

To test whether Kevin is avoiding the assignment because it is simply not interesting to him, the teacher would make the assignment more contextually relevant by incorporating something Kevin finds interesting.

For example, if the assignment involves multiplication and division of decimals and fractions and the teacher knows that Kevin likes baseball, she could ask him to name his ten favorite baseball players, past and present. The teacher would then go to the internet and search the statistics for each baseball player. Next, she would create a worksheet listing the names of each player in the first column, the number of times the player went up to bat in any given season in the second column, and the number of hits the player got that season in the third column. In the fourth column, Kevin would be instructed to calculate each player's batting average. If he stops, misbehaving, attends to the teacher, and is engaged in the task once the assignment has been modified, then the escape hypothesis is proven correct.

On the other hand, if Kevin continues to misbehave, the escape and attention hypotheses cannot be confirmed. In that case, the behavior may serve a power/control function.

Testing for Power/Control

There is a consensus among social psychologists that most human interactions involve power dynamics. In fact, power dynamics should be considered when examining any social interaction, wherever it may take place. Sometimes power is related to control. For example, the person with power promotes his or her own goals by exerting influence over the actions of others without their consent, against their will, or without their knowledge or understanding. In this context, power is defined as the ability to produce social influence.

The behaviors of students who are motivated by power/control issues can be especially challenging and disruptive. Performing a functional analysis for power/control is different from the traditional approaches used previously to test for attention and escape/avoidance. Testing for power/control involves a "ruling out" process. Take the example of Justin, a third grader prone to making disruptive animal noises. Remember, if a teacher is testing for power/control, she already tested for attention and escape using approaches described previously for Kevin and none of the manipulations resulted in Justin's misbehavior decreasing. Testing for power/control begins by "ruling out" escape.

Ruling Out Escape

Ruling out escape is quite easy and provides additional information regarding power/control. In this case Justin is alternately tapping his pencil or has his head down on the desk when he is suppose to be working on a math assignment. Unlike the traditional way to test for escape by altering the task, the teacher is going to determine a high interest activity Justin likes to perform. This is quite simple: All the teacher has to do is think of what Justin likes to do when he has free time or the behaviors he engages in instead of working on math. It is known that one of Justin's favorite activities is to draw. The teacher would get a nice drawing pad and the type of markers Justin likes and present the activity this way:

> *Justin, during math, I'm going to give you a direction that I absolutely demand that you follow. That direction is that you will draw whatever you want for the remainder of the period!*

That direction sounds very peculiar and strange. But it is simply ruling out escape, not letting Justin avoid math from then on. The idea is that if Justin wants to escape math, he would gladly follow the teacher's direction and spend the class period drawing. On the other hand, if he says, "No way am I doing that" or says nothing and puts head on the desk, the teacher can rule out escape. The idea is for the teacher to provide the direction in a demanding fashion. The reason is to bring out any power/control issues with Justin by being confrontational yet the direction is to engage in a desirable behavior. If Justin puts his head down, he is communicating to the teacher that although he finds drawing reinforcing, he finds it more reinforcing to resist the teacher's direction. The next step is to rule out attention.

Ruling Out Attention-Seeking

Just like ruling out escape, the "rule-out" for attention is different than "testing" for attention, described previously. This type of "rule-out" involves changing some aspect of the context surrounding the behavior. Recall Principle Three from *Chapter 1: Context Gives Behavior Meaning*, and changing or manipulating the context surrounding a behavior sets off a domino effect that alters meaning, purpose, and the desire to perform behavior, thus rendering the behavior useless, (i.e., non-functional). Context can be manipulated in four ways:

1. Change the time (when the behavior occurs);

2. Change the location (where the behavior occurs);

3. Change the topography/appearance (what the behavior looks like);

4. Change the frequency/amount (how often the behavior occurs).

In the case of Justin making animal noises, one way the teacher could change the context would be to encourage him to keep making animal noises. For example, saying, "Justin, you are getting quite good at making animal noises, but I bet that with more practice, you can get even better!" The teacher would then encourage Justin to spend two minutes at the beginning of each class practicing animal noises. This manipulation involves changing the time. Previously, he made animal noises whenever he wanted. Now, he is allowed (and instructed) to make animal noises at a specific time—two minutes at the beginning of each class.

Justin's response to the change in context will provide evidence of his motives for misbehaving. If making animal noises is a way for Justin to get attention, then he will most likely take advantage of the new context and continue to make animal noises now that he is being encouraged to do so. If, on the other hand, Justin refuses to make the noises when encouraged by the teacher to do so, then his behavior is probably motivated by power/ control. In this case, changing the context not only proved the teacher's hypothesis, but also had the effect of stopping Justin's disruptive behavior! This result indicates that Justin finds the feeling of power/control derived from refusing to follow the teacher's directions more reinforcing than the fun of making animal noises.

The teacher could also change the context by manipulating the location where the behavior occurs. This would entail directing Justin to only make animal noises at a specific place, such as a designated "animal noise chair" or certain area of the classroom. If the teacher no longer objects to Justin making the noises and he is no longer able to push her buttons, Justin will no longer be able to derive a sense of empowerment or control through this behavior. If, on the other hand, he is seeking attention, he is likely to follow the new directions and make the noises at the designated chair.

To change the topography, the teacher could instruct Justin to add a physical component to the behavior. For example, the teacher could say, "Justin, your animal noises are getting really creative, but next time, I want you to flap your arms if you're quacking or pant if you're barking." If he is seeking attention, Justin will be happy to make even more of a scene by acting out the part of different animals. On the other hand, if he is engaging in a power struggle with the teacher, he will refuse to follow the new instructions.

Finally, to change the amount/frequency of the behavior, the teacher could instruct Justin to perform the behavior more often. When experimenting with changing the frequency of a behavior, teachers should encourage students to increase rather than decrease the frequency of behaviors. If the teacher were to tell Justin to perform the behavior less frequently, he would probably resist, either because he really wants to engage in the behavior (to gain attention or because it's fun), or because he is intent on disobeying instructions in order to gain power/control. However, if he is instructed to engage in the behavior more often, his response makes his motives more clear. If he stops making the noises or makes them less often, then it is likely he is simply being disobedient for reasons of power/control (after all, he wouldn't suddenly stop liking the attention or finding the behavior to be fun).

In each of the examples above, if the function of making animal noises is to gain attention, Justin will have no problem following the modified directions because in each case doing so would result in him obtaining more attention. Conversely, if he refuses to follow the directions, then the power/control hypothesis can be confirmed.

It's important to realize that the inappropriate behavior may not stop or decrease in response to these context-changing techniques. But even if the inappropriate behavior continues, these manipulations should not be deemed a failure. Not succeeding and failing are two very different things. A technique may not succeed in so far as it may not produce the desired outcome; even so, it will not have failed because it at least provides the teacher with more information and insight into what to try next.

> **Trying and failing is not failing, it's assessment.**
> **Never trying is failing.**

Conclusion

This chapter focused on what all adults know at some level: That behavior is purposeful. Even reflexive behavior is purposeful. For example, if someone claps his hands close to your face, you blink. The goal is for teachers to engage in activities and manipulations designed to determine the purpose and, by so doing, address problem behaviors more effectively.

All too often, teachers react to the problem behavior and fail to determine the purpose it serves. Reacting to problem behavior typically results in noncompliance and a power struggle. However, when teachers observe challenging behaviors instead of reacting negatively, they should go into "detective" mode to try and determine their purpose. This approach takes the teacher out of "react" mode and into problem solving mode which is more likely to encourage appropriate behaviors and less resistance from students.

Teachers can think of inappropriate behavior as nothing more than a deviant form with a non-deviant intent. Sounds cryptic? Not really. Children misbehave (form) in all sorts of ways to get attention (intent) from others. But is there anything wrong with wanting to obtain attention from others? Of course not. All humans engage in behaviors to get attention from others such as eye contact, smiling, saying "hi," or telling a joke. Are there appropriate versus inappropriate ways for students to get attention? Absolutely. That's why it's so important to teach students "replacement behaviors" as was described in Principle 2 from chapter 1. A replacement behavior is an appropriate behavior that serves the same purpose as the inappropriate behavior.

All to often, teachers simply want students to stop behaving badly. However, this approach leaves a void that must be filled. For example, if a student makes animal noises to get her teacher's attention, then she must be taught an appropriate way to get the teacher's attention such as raising her hand and waiting to be called on. Nothing could make such simple sense, yet it is rarely understood or acknowledged by teachers. Think about it: if you have a flat tire, do you simply take the tire off and drive away or do you replace it with the spare?

If a light bulb burns out, do you remove it and assume that the lamp will now work or do you replace the burned out bulb with a new one? When an old battery no longer powers a flashlight, do you remove it and assume the flashlight will work fine or do you replace the old battery with a new one? When the cartridge in your printer runs out of ink, do you remove it and continue to use the printer or do you replace it with a new cartridge? There are so many everyday examples of replacement behaviors. But when it comes to students, we often assume that by simply "removing" the bad behavior that good behavior will automatically occur. It won't. Furthermore, a student will simply shift from one inappropriate behavior to another in order to get his needs met. Teachers who understand this perspective, engage in the activities involved in functional assessment, and teach students replacement behaviors are better abie to effectively handle oppositional behavior and stay out of power struggles.

Chapter 7
Manipulating the Context

Like any good magician or comedian, manipulating context makes it impossible for someone to view any particular experience in the same way. What makes a punch line of a joke effective is when it takes us in an entirely different direction than what we thought. Magicians manipulate context to focus our attention away from the salient aspects of a trick and then bring our focus back after the manipulation has occurred. Just like good comedians or magicians, teachers can manipulate context to obtain a change in students' behaviors. The reason is because when the context surrounding a behavior is altered, so too is the meaning, purpose, and the desire to perform the behavior, thus rendering the behavior potentially useless.

The last chapter presented techniques for manipulating context in order to rule out escape and attention, and confirm power/control as the primary function of a student's misbehavior. The same approaches can be used to deal with a variety of challenging behaviors. However, using context-changing techniques to obtain a change in a student's behavior is uniquely audacious. It is important to understand that any of these techniques can be modified in an almost endless number of ways to fit a teacher's particular classroom, students, and situation. Consequently, the more creative teachers can become in making modifications, the greater the number of situations for which these techniques can be applied.

"I Bet You Can Get Even Better At Swearing"

Swearing can be addressed by instructing a student to do more of it. Suppose a teacher has been unsuccessful at eliminating a student's swearing, having tried numerous negative consequences including sending him to the principal's office and conferencing with his parents (his father says he doesn't know "what the hell the goddamn problem is"). The student is quite aware that his teacher doesn't like his swearing and believes she can't do anything to stop it. It is at this point where context-changing techniques, regardless of how peculiar they may sound, may be successful. A teacher could approach this problem the following way:

> *You sure are swearing a lot in my class. And I've been unable to get you to stop. That reminds me of a student I had a couple years ago with a similar problem. I once counted that he swore 256 times in one week during class. You know, that gives me an idea. I'm going to write the number 256 on the chalkboard. Then I'll make a tally mark every time you swear to see if you can break his record by the end of the week.*

The student is caught in a double-bind—which is exactly the goal! If he swears more than 256 times—a daunting task even for a quick talker— he is following the teacher's direction and therefore is being compliant. Granted, the goal of getting him to stop swearing has not yet been reached. But teachers shouldn't lose faith and give up. The reason is because when compliance is obtained in one area, it becomes easier to do so in other areas. Even if the student refuses to follow the teacher's request to swear, compliance is nevertheless obtained. The student may think he's figured the ploy and respond by saying, "That reverse psychology stuff won't work on me." Regardless, the result is the same—he stops swearing. A logical follow-up response to the student might be, "Oh gosh, I knew you were much to smart to fall for that stuff."

Teachers who work in a pubic school may think that this technique goes way beyond the audacious and in fact, borders on being unethical. After all, what principal or parent who is visiting a classroom or even walking by it would endorse its use? Therefore, here is a viable modification.

In order to be in observance with school policy, a teacher can first remove the student from the classroom when he swears. However, when class is over, the teacher can engage him in the following dialogue:

> *I had no choice but to remove you from the classroom when you swore. It's one of the school rules and I don't have any authority to change it. But I also know how much you enjoy swearing in my classroom—especially in front of me. So here's my idea. When I have some free time, I'll get you from whichever activity or class you're in, we can go to my classroom, and you can swear for 30 minutes.*

It's crucial that when first talking to the student after class, the teacher does so in a nonchalant way. She should not sound stern nor punitive. Such an attitude will only give the student power and control, as he notes the reaction. By exuding a matter-of-fact attitude that indicates being pleased that the student has an opportunity to swear, the teacher eliminates a power struggle and takes some of the fun out of the situation for the student.

It's important for the teacher to approach the student while he is engaged in a high-preference activity such as art class, P.E., lunch, computer time, or recess. The reason is to increase the likelihood that he will say "No" to going to the teacher's classroom. Saying "No" reverses the context surrounding the behavior because the teacher is normally telling him to stop swearing and he refuses. Now he's refusing to swear—exactly the desired goal! The teacher can then say, "Okay, that's not a problem. I'll come and get you again when I have more free time to see if you want to swear in my classroom." If, on the other hand, the student agrees to swear, then he is being compliant with the direction. In that case, the teacher can sit across the student in the classroom, set a kitchen timer for 30 minutes, and tell him to begin swearing. It won't take more than 30 seconds before he tires. When this happens, he can be encouraged to continue. If he refuses, he can be told that it's okay and he can try again another time to do 30 minutes of swearing.

Here's another unique modification: changing the topography surrounding the behavior. The teacher can make a game out of swearing by telling the student she will permit him to swear in the classroom as many times as he wants, as long as he wants, and to whomever he wants.

The only stipulation is that he use swear words that have a long vowel. There are very few, if any, conventional swear words that have long vowels in them. The closest you can get is the less offensive "a-hole" for "asshole." To follow up, the student could be encouraged to make up his own swear words using long vowels and give them any designation he wants. In this way, he is swearing without swearing.

"Throw Your Tantrum Now!"

Dealing with students who tantrum, argue, whine, make animal noises, swear, or engage in just about any misbehavior that is not dangerous to self or others can be addressed by changing the time the behavior occurs. This technique works well when other traditional methods have failed. In the case of tantrums, it not only can help students stop tantruming but also teach them self-control.

The traditional method for teaching students to control their temper outbursts typically involves helping them become aware of low-level cues that signal the onset of a tantrum, for example, sweaty palms, clenched jaws, knotted stomach, or negative self-talk. The goal is to help students get the tantrum under control before it becomes full-blown. However, students can also be helped to gain self-control by telling them to begin the tantrum before it usually occurs. This direction—as all context-changing techniques— places students in a double-bind. If they begin tantruming, they have proof that the tantrum is under their control, and if they refuse to tantrum, the also have proof that the tantrum is under their control because they consciously decided to not tantrum.

Here is an example of how this technique can be implemented, by admitting defeat and thereby "one-downing" the student—a state opposite of a power struggle:

> *You've been throwing a lot of tantrums lately, and I can't get you to stop. So, why don't you throw your tantrum right now instead of waiting until later. I think this idea is pretty good. After all, if you throw your tantrum now, you can get it over with. Also, throwing it now will give you more time to get really good at tantruming.*

This audacious approach may cause others to question a teacher's judgment. But if a teacher is using this technique, it's because traditional approaches have failed and the student has continued to throw tantrums. Therefore, a teacher has nothing to lose because the tantrums have continued despite her best efforts.

As with all context-changing techniques, the student's mind-set is altered. He is accustomed to not following directions and instead throwing tantrums. But if he refuses to throw a tantrum when requested, a new frame of reference has been created—one in which he is refusing to throw a tantrum which is exactly the desired response.

> ### *Modify this time-changing approach for almost any misbehavior.*

Changing the time can work for almost any behavior. Here is an example using arguing, but it could also be used for whining:

> ### Arguing
> *I'm going to give you a direction that I know you don't want to follow and that you'll think is really dumb. Usually you argue about not wanting to follow a direction and I've been unable to get you to stop arguing. So, I want you to argue with me now before I give you the direction.*

There are several important aspects to how this direction was delivered. First, by telling the student he's going to receive a direction he doesn't want to follow, the teacher is acknowledging the obvious. It builds rapport. After all, how can the student respond? He wouldn't say, "I like following all your directions." Second, saying that the direction will be "really dumb" not only continues to build rapport but also beats the student to the punch. Many students, upon being given a direction, respond by saying, "That's dumb." So, if the student eventually says "That's dumb," the teacher can respond by saying, "I told you it was dumb." This response continues to build rapport because there is nothing for the student to resist. If the student follows the direction and argues, he's being compliant. Plus, it's really difficult to argue before you want to. If the student says, "No, you can't make me argue," then he's refusing to argue and is also compliant.

"Go Sit in the Do-Nothing Chair!"

The do-nothing chair is a way of changing the location for students who passively refuse to do any work. It will work if students are passively refusing to do anything as a way to gain power and control—known as being "passive-aggressive." It will not work if they want to escape or avoid some task—perhaps because they don't possess the requisite skills for completing the assignment or think the assignment is boring. As indicated in the previous chapter, it's relatively easy to rule out escape: Give the student an easy, high-interest activity to do instead of the usual assignment. If the student performs the activity, then passivity  may serve an escape or avoidance function because it was eliminated when the opportunity to engage in an alternative activity was presented. However, if the student continues to do nothing when presented with an easy, high-interest activity, then the reinforcing value of obtaining power and control outweighed the reinforcing value of engaging in something fun. In the latter case, the do-nothing chair may be a viable approach. There are three simple logistics for using the do-nothing chair.

1. Designate a chair as the do-nothing chair.

2. Do not associate the do-nothing chair with time-out or punishment.

3. Do not put a time limit on how long a student stays in the do-nothing chair.

The designated chair may be another color or type of chair from those typically used in the classroom, or it can have a sign—anything the teacher would find acceptable. It's important to convey to students that the do-nothing chair is not punishment. The goal is not to punish students for doing nothing. Rather, teachers want to communicate that they are pleased that students have an opportunity to get really good at doing nothing. Finally, it is important to never place a time limit on how long students remain in the do-nothing chair. Doing so only gives them power and control because they can either leave the chair before time expires or stay in the chair after it expires.

In response to a student who passively refuses to complete an assignment, the teacher would causally instruct him to take a seat in the do-nothing chair. As in all context-changing techniques, it is important not to express anger, irritation, or frustration at the student's passivity. Displaying these emotions merely reinforces his passivity because he can obtain power and control by "pushing the teacher's buttons." It is equally important for the teacher to avoid appearing sarcastic, because sarcasm is often a verbal display of anger, irritation, or frustration. Here is how a teacher might present the do-nothing chair:

> Lawrence, I see that you are doing nothing instead of working on your math assignment. I've also noticed that you usually do nothing when given other assignments, and I can't stop you from doing nothing. You certainly are getting good at it. But I think you can get even better at doing nothing. The reason is because we have the do-nothing chair where you can sit and practice getting even better at doing nothing. I'm confident that you will get better at doing nothing because I have seen how good you have gotten at other tasks you practice repeatedly, such as shooting free throws in basketball.

From the previous examples for swearing, tantruming, and arguing, the same three salient points appear here:

1. By admitting failure, you avoid a power struggle because if the student agrees then compliance is reached and if the student disagrees, he is forced to say, "Yes, you can get me to stop doing nothing."

2. By conveying the direction in a very casual way, the power and control he otherwise would obtain from pushing a teacher's buttons is reduced or eliminated.

3. By linking the idea of practicing doing nothing to practicing something the student enjoys (shooting free throws), the teacher is recasting the idea of practice into something the student doesn't want to refuse.

These reoccurring themes can be applied to any behavior problem in which a context changing technique is indicated. Nevertheless, any intervention can hit snags. Therefore, here are the three most commonly asked questions regarding the use of the do-nothing chair.

1. What do I do if the student goes to the do-nothing chair and starts making noises?

This problem is actually a good one to have. Now the student is doing something and when a teacher can get a student to do something in one area it becomes easier to get a student to do something in another area. It also provides information that the purpose the behavior served was not power/control but rather attention. In that case, the teacher could walk up to the student and in an apologetic manner say,

I'm really sorry. I made a mistake. I thought you wanted to get better at doing nothing. But I can see there are lots of things you want to do such as making animal noises or doodling. So, why don't you come with me and I can give you something to do.

2. What do I do if other students say, "Hey that's not fair. How come Lawrence gets to sit in the do-nothing chair? I want to sit there too."

The teacher would approach those students and say,

> You're right, that's not fair. But right now it's Lawrence's turn to sit in the do-nothing chair. But don't worry. When I have some free time I'll let you sit in the do-nothing chair too.

As was the case when dealing with swearing, the teacher approaches the student when the student is engaged in a high-preference activity such as lunch, recess, computers, or P.E. The teacher lets her know that she has free time for her to sit in the do-nothing chair. The reason for the timing is to increase the likelihood of the student saying, "No, I don't want to sit in the do-nothing chair now." The message that's conveyed to the student is that she better be careful what she wishes for because she may just get it. In that case, the teacher can respond by saying:

> That's okay if you don't want to sit in the do-nothing chair now. I'll come and find you when I have another plan period or when I have some free time this week to see if you're ready then.

Recall Principle 7 from Chapter 1: One Size Does NOT Fit All? This principle can be used with the do-nothing chair. Here is a follow up way to respond if the teacher had begun the year telling students they will all be treated differently because they are all unique in their own way:

> Here is a perfect example of how I may treat you differently because of your uniqueness. See that chair over there? That's a very special chair. Sometimes, for some of you, it is the do-nothing chair where you can go to get really good at doing nothing. Other times it may be the whining or arguing chair. Still other times, it's the positive recognition chair where you get to sit when you do something especially well or help another student.

The teacher now has a chair that is not associated with punishment or time out and that can serve different purposes depending on the students and the behaviors they display.

3. What do I do if the student refuses to go to the do-nothing chair but continues doing nothing?

As stated toward the beginning of Chapter 1, all students communicate how to deal with them effectively through their verbal and nonverbal behaviors: teachers must astutely and patiently observe them. Put another way: Teachers should take what students give them. By doing so, the teacher can point out the following:

> Remember when I told the class at the beginning of the year how this chair is special because sometimes it's the do-nothing chair, other times it's the whining or arguing chair, and still other times is can be the positive recognition chair? Well, this chair has another special feature: It can float around the room so that any chair can become the do-nothing chair. And since you refuse to move to the do-nothing chair, it moves to you so now you're sitting in it.

As indicated several times previously, it is important to deliver this information to the student in a nonchalant fashion so that it doesn't come off as being sarcastic. By doing so, the teacher has altered her communication based on what the student communicated. Instead of getting into a power struggle trying to get the student to the do-nothing chair (which would defeat the purpose since it then would come across as punishment), the teacher is accepting the student's resistance and modifying her response accordingly.

Use of the do-nothing chair is an example of changing different aspects of the context. The chair is in a different location—whether the designated chair or the chair the student is currently sitting in and refusing to leave. The amount of doing nothing is also changed. The student will either start doing something sooner than he usually does or stay in the chair longer. The do-nothing chair can also be used to change the time. The teacher may preempt a student who has difficulty getting to work and instead does nothing. She may say:

> *I know that during math class you like sitting and doing nothing. As you know, we have the do-nothing chair for situations like this. So, please sit in the do-nothing chair before math so you can get a head start.*

Like all of the context-changing applications described thus far, the student is caught in a double-bind. If he goes to the chair, he's being compliant and also changing the routine of doing nothing. If he refuses to sit in the do-nothing chair, he's now communicating that he won't do nothing which is the opposite of what he normally says and does.

"Look at Me—I'm a Coyote"

One way to address students who make animal noises is to change the topography—or physical appearance of the behavior. For example, with a student who persists in howling like a coyote, a teacher might respond in the following way:

> *Clyde, you seem to enjoy howling like a coyote. But you really don't look much like a coyote howling in your chair. Why don't you get down on your hands and knees, point your head at the ceiling, and really howl away.*

If the student refuses to howl, then the ultimate goal has been achieved. But if the student follows the direction, compliance momentum has been initiated. Also, any unwanted attention the student may have received from making animal noises is eliminated by giving him a stage from which to misbehave. In addition, if the student follows the teacher's direction, the attention is now deliberate and desired because he's being compliant. Depending on the particular student and situation, the teacher can have another student be a "clap-o-meter" to measure which day Clyde makes the best animal noises.

An important consideration when using this technique is to ensure the student is not embarrassed nor for it to appear that the teacher is bullying him. As such, the teacher is always requesting that the student engage in the behaviors. The student is never forced to get down on all fours and howl. If a teacher actually had that type of power, she probably could have gotten the student to stop howling a long time ago. If the student refuses to follow the direction for whatever reason, the goal of getting him to stop howling has been reached. Similarly, if he follows the direction, he is being compliant. The direction can then be modify by instructing him to sit (or crawl) in the "animal-noise" chair or select a different time for him to howl, perhaps directly before beginning a lesson.

"You Can Get Even More Creative with Your Lying"

Lying is a behavior that drives everyone crazy. Parents often tell their children that if they tell the truth, the punishment won't be as severe. From the child's perspective, lying may result in not getting punished at all. Although this childish thinking may not always work, it does point out that one of the purposes lying serves is to escape or avoid an unpleasant consequence. The other major purpose lying serves is to gain attention. A student can sometimes tell such outrageous and blatant lies that teachers often frown while peers just roll their eyes. These reactions just serve to reinforce the student's behavior through the attention he receives. The following is an example of a contextual approach that changes both the amount and time lying occurs:

Annie, you're getting really good at lying (If the student says, "No I'm not; I never lie," you can respond "See, I knew you were getting good at lying.") But I think you can get even better and more creative. Here's my idea. I'm going to approach you ten different times today and ask you a very simple question and I want you to give me the most outrageous answer you can. So, I may come up to you while you are at the library sitting by a window and say, 'Annie, what color is the sky?' And I want you to answer with the most outrageous thing you can think of such as, 'It's purple with pink polka dots'."

Some students, when asked this question, will say, "That's stupid, of course the sky is blue!" In that case, the pattern of lying has begun to reverse because the student is now telling the truth. Even if the student comes up with a more outrageous answer, the lying has been turned into a caricature which tends to give the student perspective on the silliness of her lying.

Summary

The techniques presented in this chapter were based on changing the context surrounding a behavior. The amount, the time, the location, or the appearance can be changed. Several manipulations can also be incorporated together for addressing the type of behavior problems presented.

Swearing: change the amount (swear 265 times); change the time (get the student when engaged in a high preference activity to swear);

Tantruming: change the time (throw your tantrum now, why wait); change the location (special place in room to tantrum);

Arguing: change the time (argue before being given an instruction); change the amount (argue for 20 minutes);

Doing Nothing: change the location (have a do-nothing chair); change the time (do nothing now and get it out of your system);

Animal Noises: change the time (make your animal noises now), change the location (section of the room reserved for making animal noises); change the topography (have the student pantomime the animal);

Lying: Change the time (request the student to lie at random times during the day) change the amount (lie 25 times today).

It is important to remember that these techniques are based on two assumptions. First, the behavior must not be dangerous to the student or others. The reason is because the student will initially be permitted to engage in the behavior under different situations. Second, the teacher must be able to at least initially tolerate the misbehavior occurring. An inappropriate behavior can't be eliminated unless it's performed at a different time, location, topography, duration or frequency.

Chapter 8
Embracing Uniquely Audacious Interventions: The Last Resort!

The wide-ranging interventions described in the preceding chapters have a strong track record of success, helping countless teachers manage students who display challenging and oppositional behaviors. However, there is no guarantee such strategies will work with all students, such as those who have the most severe behavioral problems. Sometimes, for these students, truly audacious and atypical techniques are required. These last resort techniques focus primarily on manipulations that reframe or recast behaviors to change their meaning.

What is Reframing?

Reframing involves modifying a person's perception or view of a situation or behavior. Reframing takes place in many fairy tales and fables: the strange-looking duckling turns into a swan, Rudolf the Reindeer's shiny red nose becomes a useful beacon guiding Santa's sleigh on a foggy night, and so on. Many teachers informally use reframing by trying to get students to think about things differently or see things from a different point of view. The goal is for students to respond differently to familiar situations.

Reframing is based on the notion that inappropriate behaviors are only inappropriate in certain contexts. In different settings or situations, inappropriate behaviors may be perfectly appropriate. For example, in the classroom it is inappropriate for a student to respond to directions by saying, "You can't make me." However, this response would be commendable if the student was being pressured by peers to drink, smoke, or engage in other destructive behaviors.

A person's frame of reference also influences whether a certain behavior is perceived as appropriate or inappropriate. Therefore, changing one's frame of reference can result in a change in perception, causing a behavior that was previously considered inappropriate to be considered appropriate. For example, a teacher who has been unable to get a difficult student to comply with directions could adopt a new frame of reference that changes the perception or meaning of the student's behavior, such as reframing "stubbornness" as the positive quality, such as "persistence." When seen in a different light, a student can no longer continue engaging in the behavior as it was previously, because the interpretation has been changed. A person's interpretation of an event leads to what behaviors are selected and engaged in at any given time.

In this chapter reframing techniques are provided along with specific examples for a variety of behavior problems including arguing, stealing, justifying behavior, and making excuses. Reframing approaches tend to be less formal than other techniques. However, they can easily be incorporated with any of the other techniques presented in this book when the situation dictates.

Revisiting Arguing: The Making of a Politician

Students who enjoy arguing are usually bright, often engaging, and tend to derive more satisfaction out of irritating teachers than pleasing them. Usually, students' arguing is not actually aimed at convincing adults of anything. Rather, arguing feels good for them because it discharges pent-up emotional energy and provides feelings of power and control.

Some students are very adept at drawing teachers into arguments. It may be futile to try to convince such students that their position is wrong. Students who enjoy arguing operate like politicians involved in a debate. Their goal is not to change the other politician's mind, but rather to catch him or her in a lie or blunder and "score points" with voters. Similarly, students like to catch teachers in some faux pas and then point out the inconsistencies of the teacher's position. For these types of students, it is useful to reframe arguing as debating. The teacher would begin by saying something like,

> *You're really good at arguing and I haven't been able to get you to stop.*

This comment puts the student in a double bind. If he nods his head affirmatively and says to the teacher, "Yeah, you got that right," then he's not arguing with the teacher anymore. This constitutes a subtle form of reframing in which the teacher demonstrates to the student that he doesn't have to challenge everything the teacher says. On the other hand, the student could choose to argue with the teacher and says, "No, I'm not good at arguing—I don't know what you're talking about." In this case, the teacher would try to convince him that he really is good at arguing. Doing so may coax the student into an argument about how he's not good at arguing. The teacher would point out this contradiction to the student, saying,

> *Gosh, you sure seem good at arguing with me about how you're not very good at arguing.*

Whether the student agrees he is good at arguing or challenges that assertion (thereby demonstrating that he is indeed good at arguing), he ultimately learns that he is a good arguer. To complete this reframing, the teacher would tell the student,

> *You know, being good at arguing is a skill that not everyone has. Politicians, talk show hosts, and TV analysts are good at arguing because they can get their points across convincingly.*

Through this statement, the teacher reframes the perception of what it means to be argumentative. Rather than being a bad quality, being argumentative can now be associated with a valued communication skill.

The teacher and student are in agreement because they are now "speaking the same language." The student's behavior no longer has the ability to frustrate the teacher and, consequently, he is less likely to engage in it because it doesn't get him what he originally wanted. The teacher could follow up by encouraging the student to join the debate team, where his propensity for arguing could be an asset. Or the teacher could follow up by using one of the context changing techniques from the previous chapter, such as giving the student a set time or location to argue with the teacher.

Stealing: The Making of a Detective

Stealing is a difficult problem for teachers to deal with. Not only is the behavior inappropriate, but it also evokes strong value judgments. Even the Ten Commandments state, "Thou shall not steal!" Teachers are often morally (and visibly) offended when students steal. To make matters worse, students who steal often lie—another behavior associated with immorality—to cover up their behavior. When teachers become upset over students stealing and lying, they end up exacerbating the problem because students often enjoy getting a rise out of their teachers. Furthermore, when teachers are fixated on value judgments, they are not focused on helping students eliminate the behaviors.

Obviously, stealing is a behavior for which context changing techniques such as those presented in the previous chapter would not be indicated. It would be unethical (and counterproductive) for a teacher to give the student a set time to steal or a certain amount of objects to steal. Therefore, the following reframing example may be helpful. It may also help teachers overcome moral indignation related to stealing.

Teachers can achieve a different perspective—both for themselves and students—by considering the skills required of a good thief and liar: being observant, organized, meticulous, strategic, quick, creative, evasive, and usually very smart. These are skills that are generally considered attributes. When teachers become cognizant of these valued skills, they reframe the context in which they perceive the student and the behaviors.

The teacher must also help the student reframe his own perception of his behavior and, more broadly, his self-image. This can be achieved by pointing out to the student the positive skills associated with the behaviors and letting him know that most successful people have mastered these strategic skills. It is also helpful to give the student a project that will require him to use these skills towards a positive end. The following is an example of a project that could be given to a student who steals and lies.

> *Teacher: Jane, I've noticed you've become pretty good at stealing and then lying to cover it up. I'm impressed because this requires you to be very observant, organized, detailed, quick, creative, and persuasive. But you and I both know that lying and stealing are wrong, and I can't allow it in this classroom. However, there is another way we can make use of your talents. It seems we are always losing things here at school: pencils, papers, student projects, cleaning supplies, and the like. I think you would be able to help me find these items without anyone else knowing what you're doing. Also, visitors to the school are always coming and going, and people don't always remember to go to the office and sign in. We need to know how many people come in and out, so I'd like you to help me keep track of people visiting the school without them knowing.*

This approach could, potentially, be effective because the student is not being punished or told that she is bad; rather she is made aware of her positive skills and attributes. Even the youngest of students know that lying and stealing is bad, and those who perform these behaviors usually think poorly of themselves. This reframing technique helps the student reframe her perception of herself. In addition, the activity provides the student with a way of receiving positive attention from the teacher when she reports on her assignment, making it a win-win situation.

The Self-Justification Shuffle

Some students who misbehave attempt to justify everything they do. It is, in essence, a form of arguing or defending what they're doing. Teachers can deal with students who constantly make justifications for their inappropriate behavior by instructing them to justify some of the mundane things they do. For example, a teacher could say the following:

> *You sure are good at justifying the things you do. I want to give you a chance to get even better at doing this. This means you will have to give me three reasons today why you are wearing the clothes you have on. Tomorrow, give me three reasons why you use the route you take when walking to school. The next day, I want three reasons why you choose certain foods for lunch. And the day after that, explain three reasons for using the type of pencil or notebook you use in class. Of course, you don't have to give me only three reasons; give me as many reasons as you want. You can write them down on a piece of paper in case you want to work ahead.*

Tackling this exercise will be extremely exhausting and boring for the student, and is likely to make him not want to justify anything at all! Equally important, the student may discover that his justifications are often merely flimsy rationalizations. Therefore, this activity combines some of the context changing techniques from the previous chapter (i.e., number and type of behavior) with reframing to give the student a different perspective on his justifying.

All Excuses

As in the case for arguing and justifying, students who make excuses are trying to goad the teacher into a struggle to obtain power/control. Teachers often don't want to hear excuses yet, for example, they nevertheless ask students for reasons why

they didn't turn in an assignment. The irony is that if the teacher doesn't want an excuse for not turning in an assignment, then she shouldn't ask the question. Does it really matter whether a student makes an excuse or not if the assignment wasn't turned it? Rather, it's more beneficial for the teacher to simply deal with the fact that the student failed to turn in the assignment. However, some students make excuses even when the teacher doesn't ask for reasons why they behaved in certain ways. The following strategy is designed to help students accept responsibility for their actions. It entails instructing a student to carry out an assigned task incorrectly and then instantly offer excuses for the outcome.

> *Teacher: Joe, you sure do give me a lot of excuses for why you don't finish work or follow my directions. The last time you completed a math assignment was two weeks ago. That assignment had 25 problems on it. I'd like for you to redo that assignment, but this time make sure you answer all the questions incorrectly. Then I want you to show it to me and give me as many reasons as you can why I should not mark the questions incorrect. Perhaps the lighting was bad in the room, your math book was missing a page, or your brother was playing loud music. Of course, these are just some examples. I know you can come up with other good excuses.*

This is a lighthearted exercise, not a trick. The student will come to realize the absurdity of always making excuses rather than accepting responsibility. Or, the student will refuse to do the assignment incorrectly. Also, as in the previous examples, the teacher is no longer frustrated at the student's behavior, hence taking away the reinforcing feeling of power/control.

Denial Self

In this variation on the previous technique, a student is told to generate a list of basic facts. Once he turns in this list, the teacher instructs him to deny everything on it. This might require him to deny that she has parents, attends school, takes piano lessons, has brown eyes— even that she was born! Having to "deny oneself about himself" makes students see things in a different light. This technique can be used in conjunction with the

previous one for students who make excuses. Which one a teacher uses will depend on the situation and the specific types of excuses a student makes.

Conclusion

These techniques and the problems they are designed to address focus on changing the meaning that individuals attach to certain behaviors. This process of "reframing" is beneficial to both teachers and students. Teachers can benefit from reframing because it reduces the likelihood they will get frustrated or annoyed when students display challenging behaviors. For students, this takes a lot of fun out of the misbehavior because they no longer get the reaction they wanted in order to obtain power/control. These techniques also benefit students because they give them a different perspective from which to view their behavior. Adopting a different perspective leads to alternative interpretations and behaviors displayed in certain situations.

These techniques are highly flexible and can be adapted for a variety of situations and behaviors. They can also be used in conjunction with almost any of the other techniques described in this book, regardless of the theoretical orientation. Nevertheless, sometimes even a more outrageous approach may be warranted: Insanity!

WHEN ALL ELSE FAILS, TRY INSANITY

Why insanity? The answer is simple: A little insanity goes a long way! When teachers respond in bizarre and unexpected ways to a student who misbehaves, that student is thrown off guard; a new context that causes the student to take on a new perspective is introduced. Some of the strategies recommend in this book may seem insane, but when all else fails, they're at least worth a try. Their use is certainly much better than the alternative of giving up on the student.

Many of the audacious, atypical, even "insane" strategies described in this book are intended to disrupt students' rigid mindsets. Recall the stimulus response chain discussed in Chapter 5: a stimulus becomes a cue or prompt for a student to perform a behavior and that behavior—or other people's response to it—becomes a cue or prompt to perform another behavior, and so on. Handing out a math quiz may be a cue or prompt for a student to throw the sheet of paper on the floor. Throwing the paper on the floor becomes a cue for to the teacher to say, "Please pick up the paper," which prompts the student to say, "No, you can't make me." These types of stimulus-response sequences lead to power struggles.

But what if the teacher were to respond in an unexpected way, such as throwing the math quiz on the floor before the student has the opportunity to do so? This disrupts the usual sequence and breaks the stimulus-response chain. The student is then faced with a brief "stimulus-absent" period. This is the time at which he is most likely to following directions.

Anyone—not just teachers or mental health workers—can use surprise and shock to shape children's behavior. Parents often find this approach very helpful. The following is a particularly creative and memorable example:

> *A seven-year-old girl pitched a fit in the middle of a mall one day. It was a real floor-mopping tantrum—the child was screaming and rolling around on the floor vigorously flailing her arms and legs. Instead of being embarrassed because others were observing the scene, the mother responded by immediately dropping to the floor screaming and flailing her arms and legs. Her daughter immediately stood up, put her hands on her hips and said, "Mom, stop it. You're embarrassing me!"*

In 1983, Anne Hassenpflug wrote an article for the *English Journal* entitled, "Insanity in the Classroom." It is an apt way to end this book.

> *On that day when all the classroom management systems I had diligently absorbed in years of inservice completely collapsed, I tried insanity. As I approached the classroom, students were not doing what they were supposed to be doing, and the noise level reached an ear-piercing volume. I refused to start screaming or shouting commands and threats. I simply walked into the room, looked down at the floor as if addressing a small dog, and said, "Toto, I don't think we're in Kansas anymore." As students began to turn toward me to see what was going on, I asked one*

of the worst offenders if he would like to take Toto out into the hall to play for a while. More heads turned and more mouths shut.

The noise and activity were still out of control...I began talking to an imaginary elf (but a stuffed animal or small statue would have done as well) about the unbelievable behavior of these students. When I ran out of conversation, I started watching an imaginary wasp flying around the room. Almost everyone's eyes were on the teacher now. One particularly nasty individual, however, was still putting on a show of his own. I took my clipboard and stood by him and silently noted down everything he did as if I were an entomologist studying a new species.

Shortly, this student was so fed up that he sat down without me ever having to say a word. I sauntered over to another offender and began speaking politely in a mixture of French and German. The student turned red and sat down. Class was ready to begin now, and the preliminary calming procedures had taken only five minutes in comparison to the usual ten to fifteen of yelling.

My first attempts at insanity were so successful that I added new absurdities to my repertoire. To the student reeking of garlic who seemed to be constantly leaning on my desk and rearranging my papers, I announced that my desk had been contaminated with poison ivy. Although I was immune, I feared she might not be. She immediately backed away, and, whenever she ventured closer, I just smiled and said my magic phrase, "poison ivy."

Another girl regularly stood by my desk and whined about not wanting to work. She always demanded to know why she could not be sent to the gym instead. One day, I jumped up, slammed down my book, and walked out of the room. Upon my return in about two minutes, she was doing her assignment and never again asked to go to the gym.

On especially bad days, I just stopped talking to students altogether. Instead, I wrote commands on large sheets of paper or on the blackboard. I wrote individual notes to offenders as well, and they usually stopped talking to read their notes and then got on with the work. To divert the class's attention from ongoing incidents of misbehavior, I began pointing out the window and describing all the imaginary beings, events, and objects I saw out there. When a particularly obnoxious student started asking me questions about the assignment before I was ready to begin giving directions, I ignored the person and talked about the spaceship waiting outside for us. I gave the student the desired attention, but I hadn't allowed myself to be forced to dance to her tune.

For long-lasting effect, I developed an imaginary creature known as "Dragon Lady." Misbehaving students started getting notes from Dragon Lady delivered to their homerooms. The notes commanded individuals to do such things as return library books, stay awake during a movie, and stop bullying another student or face Dragon Lady's wrath. Dragon Lady periodically left her pencil or her paw print in the classroom as additional evidence of her existence. (p. 33-34)